Effective Minute Taking

ROB ROBSON
PHILIP DAVIS

The Governance Institute

First published 2012

ICSA Publishing Limited
Saffron House,
6–10 Kirby Street,
London EC1N 8TS

© ICSA Publishing Limited, 2018

The right of Globe Associates UK Ltd to be identified as author of this Work has been asserted by them in accordance with sections 77 and 78 of the Copyright, Designs and Patents Act 1988.

All rights reserved. No part of this publication may be reproduced, stored in a retrieval system, or transmitted, in any form, or by any means, electronic, mechanical, photocopying, recording or otherwise, without prior permission, in writing, from the publisher.

Typeset by Paul Barrett Book Production, Cambridge
Printed by Hobbs the Printers Ltd, Totton, Hampshire

British Cataloguing in Publication Data
A catalogue record for this book is available from the British Library.

ISBN 978-1-86072-729-0

Contents

Preface   v
About the authors   vi
How to use this book   vii

1 The purpose of minutes and the legal requirements   1
What are minutes?   1
What is the purpose of minutes?   2
The minutes as an accurate record: guiding principles   6
Summary   10

2 The role of the minute-taker and its challenges   11
The role of the minute-taker   11
The challenges of the minute-taking role   12
The dual role: taking notes and contributing in the same meeting   19
Summary   20

3 Meetings: Types, purpose and structure   21
Types of meeting   21
Effective and ineffective meetings   24
Meeting structure   26
The issue of formality   28
Summary   30

4 Understanding the role of the chairperson   31
Overview of the role   31
The effective chairperson   32
Summary   39

5 Developing a strategy for effective note-taking   41
The importance of a strategic approach   41
Developing your strategy: A step-by-step guide   43
Summary   50

6 The agenda   51
Benefits of a good agenda   51
Constructing a good agenda   52
Inclusion of timings   55
Any other business   56
Circulating the agenda   61
Summary   61

7 The importance of personal preparation   62
General administrative arrangements   62
Personal preparation   65
Summary   69

CONTENTS

8 Effective note-taking 70
Deciding on an approach to note-taking 71
An alternative approach 71
The 'learn' technique 72
Summary 84

9 Transforming notes into minutes 85
Techniques for streamlining the notes 85
Choosing the appropriate style of minutes 92
Summarising 94
Developing your minute-writing toolkit 97
Reference material 100
Summary 100

10 Structure, style and layout 101
The heading 102
Listing the attendees 104
Apologies for absence 106
Declarations of Interest 108
Minutes of the previous meeting 109
Matters arising 111
The main agenda items 112
Any other business 117
Date of next meeting 117
Numbering of the minutes 117
Proofreading the minutes 118
Circulating the minutes 119
Filing the minutes 120
Summary 120

11 Technology and the minute-taking process 122
The laptop 123
Recording devices 125
The use of smartpens 126
The impact of technology on the management of meetings 127
Summary 129

12 Communication skills and the minute-taker 130
The '3Vs' of communication 130
Understanding and evaluating the messages being communicated by others 132
Considering the effectiveness of your own communication 133
Active listening 135
Summary 138

13 Personal qualities of the proactive minute-taker 139
Assertiveness 139
Emotional intelligence 143
Summary 144

14 Personal skills development 145
The INFER memory aid 145
A personal development plan 147
Practice exercises for note-taking 149
Summary 150

Final thoughts 151
Appendix 1: Troubleshooter 152
Appendix 2: Checklists 163
Index 169

Preface

Picture the scene: everyone is sitting around the table waiting for the meeting to commence. The chairperson then utters those immortal words: 'Right, who's taking the minutes?' Eyes move upwards, downwards, sideways – anywhere but in the direction of the chairperson – while the mind of each attendee works overtime to manufacture a watertight defence as to why they cannot possibly be the 'privileged' one!

Does the scenario sound a little familiar? The reality is that people frequently find themselves called upon to take minutes, with little guidance on how they are expected to produce an accurate record of what took place. Ambiguous agreements, a vague agenda, interruptions and a poor chairperson are just some of the factors that can make this a daunting task. In addition, minute-takers face an uphill struggle in executing their role due to the perceptions of others. Where minute-taking is seen as a low-status administrative function which just about 'anybody with half a brain' can undertake, minute-takers will lack credibility and often fail to receive the level of support necessary to be truly effective in the role. Even when the role is perceived positively by others and undertaken by senior professionals, it will still present challenges: taking minutes is the bane of many a company secretary's life!

The truth is that minute-taking is a highly important function in any organisation. Successful minute-taking requires a professional approach and the application of a broad range of personal, interpersonal and administrative skills. The reasons why people shy away from minute-taking responsibilities, or why existing incumbents become frustrated with the role are many and varied. For example, some problems may relate to a corporate culture that fosters low-status perceptions about the person fulfilling the role. In such an environment, levels of support may be inadequate and provision of appropriate training and development non-existent. Other problems may relate to the poor running of meetings including ineffective leadership and indistinct objectives. Self-confidence issues and a lack of assertiveness on the part of the minute-taker can also play a part. Some minute-takers may lack the necessary skills due to inadequate training – or no training at all – whereas others may possess the skills, but be applying them in the *wrong way* and experiencing frustration and stress as a result.

So, are these multifarious problems insurmountable? Are minute-takers forever consigned to finding zero job satisfaction in the role? By no means! With the requisite *knowledge*, the correct *skills* and the right *attitude*, minute-takers can be empowered to tackle problems head on. Such an approach will, in time, eliminate many negative issues and minimise others, resulting in greater effectiveness and a more enriching personal experience.

Are *you* a disillusioned minute-taker? If so, you are warmly encouraged to rise to the challenge!

About the authors

This book has been written by the team at TMF Training, a group of personal and organisational development trainers with a passion for helping organisations to unlock the potential of their people. They present tailored solutions on a variety of topics in both management skills and personal skills.

TMF has been working closely with ICSA for the past ten years in providing a series of 'open' personal development one-day courses including Effective Minute Taking. For full details see www.icsatraining.co.uk

Rob Robson is a Chartered Secretary and Principal Lecturer at the University of Greenwich Business School.

Philip Davis is a director of TMF Training, for whom he develops and delivers a range of management workshops and training programmes.

The publishers would like to acknowledge the work of Archana Singh Karki who contributed to the first edition of this book.

How to use this book

The aim of the book

Effective Minute Taking is a comprehensive – yet accessible – volume, which aims to provide practical guidelines for overcoming most of the problems faced by minute takers and achieving accuracy in the minute-taking process. That process includes not just the note-taking phase and the writing up of the final minutes, but *all* the activities surrounding these key phases which are essential for a successful outcome. An area often overlooked in connection with the minute-taker's role is the need for effective *interpersonal* skills; this book includes practical tips regarding the development of these essential skills.

The book has been written primarily for people who are currently required to take minutes as part of their role and want an opportunity to reassess their minute-taking skills, those new to their roles with little experience of minute taking at meetings, and those who expect to be called upon to take minutes in the near future. So, if you are one of the above, then this book has been written especially for you! That said, the material will also be of general interest to chairpersons and other participants in meetings. For example, Chapter 4 deals exclusively with the role of the chairperson. This chapter has been written to help minute takers develop a deeper understanding of this role, to help them manage the minute-taker/chairperson relationship. However, the detailed checklist provided will be of benefit to anyone who is required to chair a meeting. So, if you are a minute-taker, please share this information with all the people who chair the meetings you minute; better still, encourage them to read the book!

It is not the purpose of this book to delve *deeply* into law and procedure of meetings in either the private or public sectors. Although *some* references are made and may be quite specific (e.g. references to the Companies Act); the book is primarily a *skills development* manual. As such, it is hoped that minute-takers working in all forms of organisation (in both the private and public sectors) will benefit from the practically oriented material and be able to apply the points made to their own situation. The recurring theme throughout the book is the encouragement to adopt a *proactive* approach towards the minute-taking role, with a view to sharpening existing skills sets and building the confidence to embrace new ideas.

Structure of the book

Following this introduction, the first four chapters address topics which provide context for the minute-taking process. These include the purpose of minutes, the purpose and structure of meetings, the role of the minute-taker and the role of the chairperson. The next six chapters chart the logical development of the minute-taking process, from initial strategy development through to the production of a set of minutes in their final form. The next four chapters examine associated topics including the use of technology and the development of interpersonal skills. Appendix 1 then deals with a selection of frequently asked questions and Appendix 2 provides a series of comprehensive reminder checklists. An overview of these chapters is provided below:

CHAPTER 1

The purpose of minutes and the legal requirements
This chapter highlights and discusses the various practical reasons why minutes are kept, including the specific legal requirements for companies. The discussion draws on both case law and statute to emphasise the critically important *evidential* nature of minutes. As the book is designed to appeal to a broad readership, it incorporates practical and legal issues relating to both the private and public sectors.

CHAPTER 2

The role of the minute-taker and its challenges
Anecdotal evidence suggests that the role of the minute-taker varies considerably from organisation to organisation. In some, the role is fairly narrowly defined, consisting primarily of taking notes at the meeting and writing up the final minutes. In others, the role is much broader, forming part of the company secretarial role and encompassing many additional administrative and organisational responsibilities.

This chapter explores the challenges minute-takers face, whether these be *organisational* (factors in the organisation environment) or *personal* (issues personal to the minute-taker). Among the issues examined is the challenge of having to take notes and contribute at the same meeting. The chapter places emphasis on the need for a proactive stance in order to maximise the effectiveness of the role.

CHAPTER 3

Meetings: types, purpose and structure
This chapter examines the various types of meeting at which minute-takers are required to take notes (e.g. board meetings, AGMs, committee meetings, consultative groups, project teams, management briefings etc).

Some of the areas discussed are: meeting structure, the level of formality or informality and the reasons why some meetings tend to be more effective than others. The purpose of the chapter is to provide readers with an idea of the minute-taking requirements with respect to each type of meeting and the challenges which are likely to be faced

CHAPTER 4

Understanding the role of the chairperson

If a meeting is going to run smoothly, an effective chairperson is essential. If the chairperson is ineffective, the job of the minute-taker can become needlessly complicated. In such a situation it may be difficult to follow the discussions and to isolate key decisions and actions. Minute-takers need an understanding of how the duties of a chairperson *should* be carried out. This will enable them to act with insight when managing the minute-taker/chairperson relationship.

The role of the chairperson is examined in respect of three separate phases: *careful planning* (before the meeting), *capability* (during the meeting) and *critical evaluation* (after the meeting).

CHAPTER 5

Developing a strategy for effective note-taking

Effective note-takers prepare well. This chapter discusses all the important areas including the need to have a full understanding of the nature and requirements of *each* meeting, including the meeting 'cycle' and identification of the unique challenges inherent in each meeting.

Minute-takers are encouraged to develop a specific strategy for each meeting involving all necessary activities which need to be carried out before, during and after the meeting and a useful tool is introduced: the 'minute-taking strategy map'.

CHAPTER 6

The agenda

Although the agenda forms the framework for the meeting, the 'quality' of this document varies considerably across and within organisations. This chapter discusses the practical value of taking the time to construct a well thought-out agenda, including the allocation of appropriate timings and the establishment of clear objectives.

Consideration is also given to the much used/much abused 'any other business' section, including an examination of its real purpose, the reasons why it tends to be misused and suggestions for managing it more effectively.

CHAPTER 7

The importance of personal preparation

For many minute-takers, the note-taking phase induces an element of fear and anxiety. Even when conditions are as favourable as they can be, the task still demands high levels of concentration and mental awareness. However, there are many things – things often overlooked – that a note-taker can do in order to aid concentration and make the overall experience more manageable and less stressful. This chapter provides some practical tips.

CHAPTER 8

Effective note-taking

The research and preparation discussed in the previous chapters (if undertaken) allows the note-taker to enter the meeting room with a degree of confidence. However, specific skills now need to be applied during the note-taking process. In this chapter the skills for effective note-taking are discussed in detail.

The topics featured include: understanding what needs to be included in the notes, creating a note-taking template, how to capture the main thrust of the speaker's argument, how to avoid writing long sentences whilst still capturing the key points, the use of alternative note-taking techniques such as visual recording and making effective use of abbreviations and 'personalised' shorthand.

CHAPTER 9

Transforming the notes into minutes

This chapter focuses on techniques for developing the set of notes taken during the meeting into the final set of written minutes, including the use of mind-mapping. Consideration is also given to appropriate writing style and use of grammar; a checklist of useful words, terms and phrases is also provided.

CHAPTER 10

Structure, style and layout

This chapter uses a number of examples to illustrate how the final set of minutes should be structured and set out. Explanations are given as to what should and what should not be included under each key heading.

Examples of numbering systems and ways to record background information, decisions and actions are also provided. Throughout the chapter, examples are given in relation to the different types of meeting, in order to provide a comprehensive overview.

CHAPTER 11

Technology and the minute-taking process

The technological revolution has touched many aspects of people's lives both professional and personal, so it seems appropriate to consider the role technology does/could play in the overall minute-taking process.

Technology is discussed in terms of its impact on the ways meetings are conducted, the taking of notes, the preparation of the minutes and archiving. This chapter is designed not simply to describe the methods but also to raise questions and prompt the reader to critically evaluate the potential advantages and disadvantages of using technology in the minute-taking process.

CHAPTER 12

Communication skills and the minute-taker

In this chapter, an examination is made of the '3 Vs' of communication (visual, verbal and vocal) and their importance to the minute-taker. First, in terms of achieving a greater understanding of contributors' comments and second, to help raise awareness of the minute-taker's own communication style – particularly important in managing relationships with the chairperson and meeting participants, in interactions either before, during or after the meeting.

The second part of the chapter is devoted to listening skills. Information is given regarding the different forms of listening and practical tips are given to assist the reader in developing more effective listening skills.

CHAPTER 13

Personal qualities of the proactive minute-taker

Throughout the book, the theme of the proactive minute-taker is to the fore. A key area in which minute-takers need to be proactive is in the development of personal qualities which will enhance their status in the eyes of others.

Areas such as developing assertiveness, building credibility, acquiring self-confidence and displaying emotional intelligence are discussed. Reasons are given as to why these areas are important and relevant to the minute-taker and practical tips for self-development are provided.

CHAPTER 14

Personal skills development

Apart from the personal qualities mentioned above, the minute-taker needs to take seriously the ongoing need for skills development, particularly with regard to note-taking. The book features many suggestions to help note-takers move away from writing too much and to acquire a more succinct form of note-taking.

However, 'old habits die hard' and success in genuinely embedding new skills sets is strongly correlated to continued practice. Therefore, this chapter describes a series of useful practice exercises to help readers embed these skills more fully.

APPENDIX 1

Troubleshooter

Appendix 1 is devoted to answering a range of frequently asked questions about the minute-taking process. For example, questions such as the following will be answered in this appendix: 'What can I do if the chairperson or other contributors change the contents of my minutes, thereby affecting their accuracy?' 'Is it ever necessary to record a contribution word-for-word, where brevity in minute-writing is the accepted norm?' 'What should I do if asked to change the minutes after they have been signed by the chairperson?' 'If an argument breaks out, should I minute it?'

APPENDIX 2

Checklists

The final part of the book provides three detailed checklists. These are designed as reminder tools for the minute-taker to ensure all essential activities have been undertaken. The checklists are presented as a series of questions and cover:

- Issues to be considered *before* the meeting
- Issues to be considered *during* the meeting
- Issues to be considered *after* the meeting.

How to make the most of the book

As with any book, there is some value in reading it from cover to cover. In this case, a full read-through would provide you with a comprehensive overview of the entire minute-taking process. So, if you have the staying power, go for it! The greater value of course comes from a deeper consideration of the material of particular relevance to you and your role and reflecting on how you can apply it.

The chapter breakdown in the previous section provides you with a helpful guide as to how the book is structured. This will help you to be selective when deciding which chapters to investigate more fully. The earlier chapters discuss topics such as the purpose of minutes, the different types of meetings and their structure and the role of the minute-taker. If you are very new to minute-taking or have yet to begin, these chapters will be worth considering in detail before moving on to the 'how-to' topics in subsequent chapters. If you are a more experienced minute-taker, the chapters devoted to the stages of the minute-taking process will provide you with the opportunity to reassess your minute-taking skills. If you are rather timid by nature and suffer from self-confidence issues then the chapter on the personal qualities of the minute-taker will be of particular help to you. So, there is something for everyone; simply choose the sections that will benefit you the most.

If the information is to help you in a meaningful way, it needs to be of *practical* value. The book is full of practical tips and examples that will help you to apply what you learn. Many of the layout and template examples are included in the chapter text itself rather than in the appendices. This approach keeps all the information relating to a topic in 'one place' thus making it easier to appreciate the link between theory and practice. Many of the chapters include specific text features; for example:

Stop and Think

In many of the chapters you will find a 'Stop and Think' box. This is a feature designed to encourage reflection on the subject matter before reading on; it is often accompanied by a practical exercise. The practical exercises can be undertaken there and then or at another convenient time. You are warmly encouraged to complete the exercises because they are useful tools to help you reflect on a particular situation and then make personal application. For example, in

Chapter 5 on developing a strategy for effective note-taking, there is an exercise which invites you to reflect on one of the meetings you minute and to jot down all the problems and challenges you face at that meeting and how you might overcome them.

Checklists

In most aspects of life, a checklist is a really useful reminder tool to ensure things get done, whether that is planning for a holiday, doing the weekly shop, managing the daily tasks at work or revising for an exam; the applications are endless! For the minute-taker, with an array of tasks and activities to perform, checklists can prove invaluable. Throughout the book, checklists are a regular feature. For example, Appendix 2 provides a series of reminder checklists covering the entire minute-taking process. In other chapters, the lists may take the form of practical tips or a series of review questions on a particular topic. Sometimes a checklist forms the basis for an entire chapter such as in Chapter 5 where a step-by-step planning process is described. As a minute-taker you are unlikely to apply all of the practical suggestions in this book in one go! Therefore, these checklists can act as a set of reminder tools as you develop in the role.

Case studies

Several of the chapters include a mini case study. These are based on the real-life experiences of minute-takers. They are used to illustrate the benefits of applying suggestions made in the text or, in some cases, to highlight difficulties that can occur when the minute-taker lacks confidence or is ignorant of the best course of action. The salient issues are then discussed in the text and the key learning points highlighted.

ICSA good practice

The ICSA has recently published a guidance document with regard to effective minute taking. This guidance is the product of ICSA's discussions with experienced minute takers, from both corporate and not-for-profit sectors. It therefore provides an up to date assessment of market practice and of some of the pitfalls that can face those taking minutes of meetings. Throughout the book, extracts from the guidance document have been included where good practice in particular areas is advised.

1
The purpose of minutes and the legal requirements

This chapter examines the purpose of minutes and why they are kept. There are many types of organisations and groups that keep minutes: large and small, public and private, profit-making and not-for-profit, incorporated and unincorporated. Many different types of meeting, both formal and informal, are also conducted within organisations. Notwithstanding these differences, minutes have a number of purposes which are generally applicable.

What are minutes?

So, what exactly are minutes? A simple definition would be: short notes from a meeting. Some examples of more expansive definitions are as follows:

- A written record of the main points discussed at a meeting.
- A written record of the main points discussed at a meeting including background information, decisions reached and actions agreed.
- A summary of the meeting, detailing decisions and actions.
- The official record of the meeting.
- A record of decisions taken at a meeting.
- An historical record of a meeting highlighting decisions taken and any actions agreed.
- A short written record from a meeting detailing its proceedings.

> STOP AND THINK
>
> Following on from the above definitions, take a few minutes to complete the following exercise before reading on:
>
> Think about meetings in your organisation where minutes are taken. Then on a piece of paper note down answers to the following questions:
>
> (a) What different purposes do the minutes have? Do the purposes vary depending on the nature of the meeting?
> (b) Are there any specific legal requirements regarding the minutes taken at these meetings?

What is the purpose of minutes?

How did you get on? You probably concluded that minutes have various purposes and were able to identify a number of them. You may also have concluded – when thinking about the variety of meeting types in your organisation – that minutes are not always required. For example, an informal discussion between colleagues would be unlikely to require any notes, let alone a formal set of minutes! Even where a meeting is held regularly, a full set of minutes may not be necessary; sometimes a short list of key action points will be sufficient, depending on the purpose of the meeting. So, what purpose do minutes have and why are they kept?

Minutes provide evidence of decisions taken

This is really the primary purpose of keeping minutes. It has been said that 'the strongest memory is weaker than the palest ink'. Distortion, confusion and reinterpretations can often occur when memory alone is relied upon – and there are times, of course, when people would rather not be reminded of realities obscured by selective memory. However, once something is put down in writing – in even the palest ink – it is very hard to dispute. This principle is particularly important in the world of business. Minutes provide the crucial evidential record of a meeting's proceedings. For this reason, the Companies Act 2006 requires that minutes be kept of general meetings and meetings of directors. Why is this so important? Well, it may be readily accepted that directors should not be negligent in the execution of their duties and responsibilities, but if a duty of care has not been exercised, how can that negligence be proven? An accurate, permanent, record of the key decisions taken can provide the needed evidence. The power of a set of minutes as an evidential tool is well illustrated in case law; for example, in *Municipal Mutual Insurance* v *Harrop* (1998) the directors claimed that a particular decision had not been taken. However, the decision had been recorded in the minutes and the directors had confirmed the minutes as accurate. They were legally bound by the decision.

The minutes, signed by the chairperson of that meeting, or of a subsequent meeting, are *prima facie* evidence of the proceedings of the meeting (*Re Indian Zoedone Co* (1884)). Notwithstanding the presumption that the minutes are accurate, it is possible to challenge their accuracy. During legal proceedings, evidence may be admitted to show that the minutes do not reflect an accurate record.

Regarding local authority meetings in the public sector – where there is a legal requirement for minutes to be kept – the same principle applies. In their law and practice manual: *Knowles on Local Authority Meetings*, Deborah Upton and Stephen Taylor state: 'Minutes that have been drawn up and entered in the minute book and signed at the same or next following meeting by the person presiding, i.e. at the meeting at which confirmation takes place, are prima facie good evidence of the proceedings: the law prescribes that any minute purporting to be so signed "shall be received in evidence without further proof".' However, in terms of challenging the accuracy of the minutes: 'it is open to anyone who wishes to do so, for good reason, to try to prove in court that the minutes are not a true record of what took place at the meeting. But the onus of proof to the contrary is on the person challenging the signed minute'.

So, minutes have power! If minutes are admissible as evidence in a court of law, then due care should be taken to ensure that they represent an accurate record. This begs the question: Is there an established and accepted format for recording the minutes? The answer is: not really and requirements will vary depending on the nature of the organisation, the particular type of meeting and the minute-taking procedure and standards specified in an organisation's governing document. For example, regarding council minutes, *Knowles on Local Authority Meetings* states:

> Council minutes can take whatever form is preferred by the individual authority or relevant officer concerned. There are certain general principles governing the drafting of minutes that should be observed ... but the principles are flexible and what matters primarily is that the minutes record clearly and concisely all decisions taken at the meeting and of the other proceedings as is necessary to give reasons to the decision-making.

Andrew Hamer in *The ICSA Meetings and Minutes Handbook* states:

> Because the primary purpose of the minutes and records is to provide evidence of the decisions taken, it is essential that they accurately record those decisions. As a rule of thumb, this means they should contain sufficient information to enable a person who did not attend to ascertain what decisions were taken.

The minutes are the official record of the meeting and constitute evidence of the proceedings. They provide proof that the meeting actually happened, discussions took place and certain decisions were reached. In line with this, the clear principle emerging from the above quotations is that the accurate recording of *decisions* is essential. The amount of background detail recorded in relation to those decisions is a matter for personal judgement and may be influenced both by internal conventions and by the nature of the meeting in question. For example, the minutes of a joint consultative committee comprising both management and employee representatives, would likely be more comprehensive in terms of background narrative than, say, the minutes of a board meeting.

In light of this, it is clear that a professional approach needs to be taken in the production of minutes. Minute-taking should be based on an agreed set of standards and principles and these are discussed a little further on in the chapter. This section has addressed the evidential nature of minutes and some broad, high-level legal requirements in terms of minute-taking. However, there are a number of *specific* questions on legal matters which minute-takers often ask regarding minute-taking procedures; some of these will be addressed in Appendix 1.

ICSA GOOD PRACTICE

The purpose of meeting minutes

The purpose of minutes is to provide an accurate, impartial and balanced internal record of the business transacted at a meeting.

The degree of detail recorded will depend to a large extent on the needs of the organisation, the sector in which it operates and the requirements of any regulator and on the working practices of the chairman, the board and the company secretary. As a minimum, however, we would expect minutes to include the key points of discussion, decisions made and, where appropriate, the reasons for them and agreed actions, including a record of any delegated authority to act on behalf of the company. The minutes should be clear, concise and free from any ambiguity as they will serve as a source of contemporaneous evidence in any judicial or regulatory proceedings.

Minutes may also be used to demonstrate that the directors have fulfilled their statutory duties, in particular by evidencing appropriate challenge in order to hold the executive to account and by showing that issues of risk and both shareholder and stakeholder impact have been properly considered.

A charity or public sector organisation may focus more on ensuring there is clear accountability visible through the minutes, in some cases having consideration of the fact that the minutes will be in the public domain. Alternatively, a regulated financial services company is more likely to focus on providing evidence of robust decision making; demonstrating that directors undertook their duties and responsibilities in accordance with both statutory and regulatory requirements and gave matters, particularly those relating to risk, appropriate consideration.

ICSA GOOD PRACTICE

Legal and regulatory framework

It is therefore important that consideration is given when preparing the minutes of board meetings to what may be appropriate or necessary, depending on the nature of the business and the circumstances, to demonstrate that the board members have observed their responsibilities to the company and complied with their legal and regulatory duties.

Board meetings are an internal matter and therefore the conduct of board meetings is governed by the organisation's constitutional documents. For example, every company must conduct its board meetings in accordance with its articles of association. Companies are free to set their own articles but many companies that have adopted new articles since 1 October 2009 will have included the provisions set out in the Model Articles prescribed by the Act in their articles. Companies with articles adopted before 1 October 2009 are likely to have included the provisions set out in Table A of the Companies Act 1985.

In other sectors, there is even less statutory prescription, although we were told that some regulators, notably the Financial Conduct Authority (FCA) and NHS Improvement (formerly Monitor), the sector regulator, have sought evidence of challenge in board minutes.

ICSA GOOD PRACTICE continued

There is considerable sectoral variation and each sector is likely to have its own code of governance or other standards, of which boards should be aware and for which they should have regard:

- Financial Services companies will need to be aware of the regulatory requirements and expectations of the FCA and Prudential Regulation Authority (PRA), including in relation to Solvency II, together with the implications of the Senior Managers Regime (SMR) and Senior Insurance Managers Regime (SIMR).
- Many companies will be affected by section 49 of the Pensions Act 1995 (setting out requirements for trustees) and the Occupational Pension Schemes Regulations 1996 (SI 1996/1715 Reg 3).
- Listed companies will need to pay attention to provision A.4.3 of the UK Corporate Governance Code.
- Charities have the joint Charity Commission and ICSA guidance CC48 on charities and meetings and guidance from the Office of the Scottish Charity Regulator (OSCR), whilst academy trusts also need to bear in mind guidance from the Department for Education and the Education Funding Agency.
- For universities, the Higher Education Code of Governance should be reviewed.
- Local government entities will need to have regard to the Local Government Act 1972(6).
- Public sector organisations are also subject to the Freedom of Information Act 2000.
- In local authorities, it is normal practice for committee minutes to be used to report their activities to the full council rather than by separate report. This can create tensions between the need to record the decisions of the meeting and the need for the full council to understand the background to those decisions.
- In the NHS there is scrutiny from NHS Improvement, the sector regulator, and the Care Quality Commission and NHS England, with focus on standing orders and conflicts of interest. All of their meetings are held in public, although some sections can be in private.

Minutes provide a point of reference for those unable to attend

Realistically, not every member of a group will be able to attend every single meeting held. The availability of the written minutes allows members who were unable to attend to acquire an overview of the entire proceedings and to ascertain the key decisions taken. This is more effective than relying solely on a *verbal* update from an attendee, which may not necessarily cover all the key points.

Of course, minutes may be intended for a broader readership than just the attendees of the meeting. Some minutes may be available for public inspection. On occasions it may be the intention to circulate minutes to a wider employee group; for example, the minutes of a joint consultative committee may be freely accessible to all management and staff within the organisation. Another example would be the findings of a project team or working group charged with investigating a particular issue of interest to all employees such as a review of health and safety standards or staff restaurant facilities. In these examples, the minutes would highlight the key issues, allowing the recipients to consider the salient points and to offer feedback.

Minutes provide a prompt to action

The minutes record all the actions arising from the decisions taken and the people responsible for carrying out those actions. Of course, an 'action' is really a *promise* to act; a commitment made to the entire group regarding the intended action. There is always the possibility of procrastination, particularly if the action has been agreed to reluctantly. Even where genuine enthusiasm to act exists, time can pass and other tasks may take precedence. Therefore, minutes are a useful reminder because they highlight all the promises made and their timescales for completion. This helps participants to focus on their obligations, knowing that they will have to report back to the entire group.

Minutes provide an aide-memoire at the following meeting

This is often achieved through the 'matters arising' section. This part of the meeting involves brief progress updates with regard to the agreed actions from the previous meeting. Therefore, the minutes create a link between the two meetings. The minutes from the previous meeting provide the basis for members to review all the issues and agreed actions ahead of time and come to the meeting prepared to inform the group of actions taken and/or progress made.

Minutes can also help in the formulation of agenda items for the next meeting. This can happen in two ways. First, the minutes may record some matters that were adjourned, or issues which clearly require further discussion. Second, a review of the previous minutes by each participant, may serve to stimulate thinking, leading to the generation of ideas for discussion topics.

Minutes provide a comprehensive historical record

Minutes provide a chronological record of the development of an organisation through the documentation of its decision-making processes. This historical record provides detail about the decisions taken and when and why they were taken. In this sense, it could be said that minutes help to promote good governance. The fact that many parts of this historical record will be accessible to a range of stakeholders, both internal and external, reminds those responsible for directing and controlling the affairs of the organisation of the need to conduct their dealings in an accountable, ethical and transparent manner. This record, of course, will not 'paint the perfect picture', it will reveal the high points and the low points, the successes and the failures, the good decisions and the poor decisions. When viewed in this way, minutes can be used to facilitate periodic critical reviews of strategy and operations and provide an opportunity to learn from past mistakes.

The minutes as an accurate record: guiding principles

If minutes are to reflect a truly accurate record then there must be a set of guiding principles which govern their production.

THE PURPOSE OF MINUTES AND THE LEGAL REQUIREMENTS

> ### STOP AND THINK
>
> The previous sections have highlighted the importance of the evidential nature of minutes; hence the need for an accurate record. Take a few minutes to complete the following exercise before reading on.
>
> Imagine that a person with no experience of minute-taking approaches you and asks for your advice on how to produce a professional and accurate set of minutes:
>
> (a) What key principles would you highlight?
> (b) What reasons would you give to underscore the importance of each of the principles highlighted?

You were probably able to identify a number of guiding principles underpinning the production of an accurate set of minutes. However, as an aid to retention, consider the following: You may be familiar with expressions such as the 'four Ps', 'the seven Ps' or the 'four Cs'; all versions of the marketing business tool known as the 'marketing mix'. But have you heard of the 'minute-taking mix'? Yes, a framework just for minute-takers comprised of 'the eight Cs'!

The eight Cs is a simple, easy-to-remember framework which provides eight guiding principles for the production of an accurate set of minutes. The key points are summarised in the table below, following which a more detailed explanation is provided for each one.

Table 1.1: The minute-taking mix (the eight Cs)

Guiding principle	Key points
Concise	Short and succinct; emphasis on decisions
Complete	All key elements of the meeting recorded
Consistent	Uniform approach to structure and style
Clear	Unambiguous; accessible; readable
Compliant	Observing set standards and conventions
Clean	Objective and 'clutter-free'
Correct	Accurate information; accurate writing
Coherent	Logical development of material

Guiding principle 1: conciseness

As a general rule, minutes should be short and succinct. A minute-taker is not a novelist! Even the most eloquent set of minutes will struggle to get a reading if they are too long. Information overload needs to be avoided. The aim is to exclude all unnecessary detail – however interesting or entertaining it may be – and focus on the key points of the discussion and the decisions.

Of course, the level of detail required may vary depending on the nature of the meeting; some meetings will require more background narrative than others. That said, the general principle still holds true for any meeting: minutes should be as concise as possible.

Guiding principle 2: completeness

Minutes need to be concise, but not at the expense of completeness. All key elements of the meeting must be recorded. The key parts of the discussion (to the appropriate level of detail), the decisions and the actions all need to be recorded; no important details should be omitted. Also, the minutes need to present a *balanced* picture in terms of the content for each agenda item. For example, if the discussion time on two of the agenda items was of similar duration, then the minutes will appear disjointed if the discussion for one of the agenda items is recorded in great detail and the other is noticeably brief by comparison.

Care also needs to be exercised to ensure that all the necessary layout details are included. For example, for a board meeting, the actual day of the meeting may be optional, but the date of the meeting is not!

Guiding principle 3: consistency

It is important to maintain consistency in terms of structure and style. Because minutes form an historical record, consistency in presentation over time helps preserve a professional image and makes it easier to compare 'like with like'. It is also important to maintain consistency *within* each set of minutes. Areas to consider are:

- Paragraph structure and length
- Use of tenses
- Sentence structures
    - Format and layout
    - Font type and size.

Guiding principle 4: clarity

In a clear set of minutes, the discussion sections are succinct and to the point, the decisions stand out and the actions are clearly identified. Achieving clarity can be a challenge; recording a discussion which constitutes a 'miniature version' of the meeting is far from easy. Minutes often lose clarity because the salient points are under-emphasised and/or less important parts of the discussion are developed in too much detail. The discussion must focus on the key points that 'frame' the decisions and actions. Even when the key points *are* highlighted, a lack of clarity may result due to vague descriptions, ambiguous phrasing, poor choice of words and unexplained technical terms and jargon.

Clarity is also impeded by poor grammatical construction and poor punctuation. At best, poor punctuation can make a sentence difficult to read; at worst, the entire meaning of the message may be lost!

It is also important to consider the needs of the readership. What may be clear for one group of people in terms of format, style and language, may be very unclear for another group. If minutes are to be genuinely accessible, it is imperative that consideration is given to the target audience.

Guiding principle 5: compliance

The minutes should comply with existing conventions and agreed standards regarding format and content. An organisation may have certain specific standards which are to be applied to the production of minutes for all meetings held within that organisation. Other standards may be specific to certain types of meeting. In any event it is important that these standards are observed. For many meetings, the primary driver may be the personal preferences of the chairperson. In such cases, there may be some latitude for the minute-taker to negotiate an agreed style and approach.

Guiding principle 6: clutter free

A 'clean' set of minutes is a 'clutter-free' set of minutes. Some inexperienced minute-takers aim to provide a step-by-step account of the proceedings. This is bad practice and results in information overload; the final document ends up looking more like a copy of *War and Peace* than a concise summary of events! However, it is not just the amount of information which clutters up a set of minutes; it is the manner in which the narrative is written. The key is to maintain *objectivity*. There is no need to record the intensity of the discussion (e.g. 'AJC made a strong emotional appeal for a revised approach') or the petty quarrels between participants.

Also, the language used in the minutes must never cause offence to the reader. It should go without saying that there is no place for the use of 'bad language' but any phrase which has the potential to shock or to make the reader feel uncomfortable must be avoided. There is also no place for the *opinions* of the minute-taker. This increases the level of subjectivity and decreases the level of professionalism. A set of minutes is not a university assignment requiring critical analysis on the part of the author!

Guiding principle 7: correctness

It is important that minutes do not contain inaccuracies. Some meetings are harder to minute than others in this regard, particularly when many facts and figures are featured in the discussion. The recording of incorrect dates, incorrect figures and incorrect names are common errors. Sometimes the error is attributable to spelling inaccuracies; at other times completely the wrong name is recorded (e.g. the name of an action taker).

A careful check should be made prior to the distribution of both the draft and final minutes. There is no justification for adopting a lackadaisical attitude due to the 'catch-all' facility of the 'Minutes of the last meeting' item. If every time this item is discussed, corrections are highlighted, there is something wrong!

Guiding principle 8: coherence

If the minutes are to stand as an accurate record of the meeting, then there needs to be some logic applied to the way the material is presented. The meeting is clearly structured around the agenda items and the minutes should reflect this. This may sound obvious, but the problem is that discussion within agenda items often veers wildly off point. Sections of the discussion which appear to have been concluded are suddenly re-opened. Even when an agenda item has been concluded, someone may return to it later in the meeting. So, the *notes* from the meeting may look a little disjointed due to the haphazard nature of the discussion. The essential point is that the *written minutes* should be logically organised around the agenda items irrespective of the order of discussion at the meeting.

ICSA GOOD PRACTICE
Style of writing

Minutes need to be written in such a way that someone who was not present at the meeting can follow the decisions that were made. Minutes can also form part of an external audit and a regulatory review, and may also be used in legal proceedings. When writing minutes, it is important to remember that a formal, permanent record is being created, which will comprise part of the 'corporate memory'. Minutes should give an accurate, balanced, impartial and objective record of the meeting, but they should also be reasonably concise. The importance of accuracy should not be underestimated as the minutes of a meeting become the definitive record of what happened at that meeting and who attended. Courts will rely on them as being conclusive evidence unless proved otherwise.

Summary

This chapter has addressed the basic question: What are minutes? Various definitions have been provided and the reasons why minutes are kept have been examined – a key reason being that they provide evidence of the decisions taken. It was also noted that, apart from providing an evidential record for legal purposes, minutes carry practical value from a business perspective. Clearly documented action points can help participants to avoid procrastination. Those unable to attend can refer to a clear record of what took place. The minutes also provide a chronological record of business activity.

The need for minutes to constitute an accurate record of the proceedings was highlighted and the key elements essential in achieving accuracy were discussed using the framework of the eight Cs.

Applying the eight Cs and achieving accuracy can present quite a challenge! For you, the minute-taker, there is much work to do before those completed minutes are finally circulated. There are a wide range of tasks to be executed prior to the meeting. Then there is the demanding note-taking process at the meeting itself, followed by the transformation of those notes into the final minutes. The next chapter discusses the role of the minute-taker in detail and addresses some common challenges.

2
The role of the minute-taker and its challenges

If you were applying for a new job, part of the application process would probably involve reading a detailed role description. The description would no doubt include a personal specification: the specific criteria regarding education, skills and attitudes deemed either essential or desirable by the recruiting organisation. You would then carefully analyse these criteria and assess yourself against them. If you felt that you matched the requirements reasonably well, you might then feel confident in applying for the post.

Picture yourself in that situation and imagine that you do apply and get the job! Initially, you would probably feel quite upbeat and looking forward to the challenge. However, when you start the job, you might find that there are hidden challenges, things you didn't expect and you need to adapt and draw on all your personal resources in order to negotiate them successfully.

Now, think for a moment about the role of the minute-taker. More often than not, there is no job description at all. Sometimes the only personal specification is that any person will do! No one discusses the skills and attitudes necessary for effective minute-taking, but everyone moans if they are not applied! Does this sound a little familiar? No wonder that many minute-takers view minute-taking as a major challenge even before they begin, let alone when the hidden challenges begin to emerge!

Do you feel that this describes you? Well hopefully things are not quite that dire, but the fact remains that minute-takers face many challenges and they need to draw on a wide range of personal resources to meet them successfully.

The role of the minute-taker

So, what *is* the role of the minute-taker? The common view is that it involves attending the meeting, taking the notes and then typing up the final minutes. Whilst these activities are central to the role, there are many others which may fall under the purview of the minute-taker. Many of these will relate to administrative tasks to be carried out before, during and after the meeting. Some minute-takers will be required just to take the notes and produce the final minutes; others may have a far broader administrative role. For some (e.g. company secretaries) minute-taking may be a clearly defined and fully integrated part of their overall role; for others it may form more of a 'fringe' activity. So, the nature and extent of the role may vary, but the key high-level activities are summarised as follows.

CHECKLIST

Key activities of the minute taker

- Undertaking preparatory administrative tasks prior to the meeting.
- Preparing the agenda in conjunction with the chairperson.
- Circulating the agenda and any accompanying papers.
- Taking notes at the meeting.
- Writing the minutes.
- Circulating the minutes.
- Filing the minutes.

It is not the purpose of this chapter either to discuss these aspects of the role in great detail, or to highlight the many other associated activities which fall under these high-level descriptors. This is because many of the chapters which follow are devoted to a detailed discussion of these areas. For example, the preparatory activities prior to the meeting will be examined in Chapter 7 and all matters relating to the agenda in Chapter 6. Also, in Chapter 5, you are invited to develop your own strategy for effective note-taking. The skills for effective note-taking will be discussed in Chapters 8 and 9 and Chapter 10 focuses on the structure, style and layout of the minutes, together with a discussion of some of the important activities to be undertaken after the meeting. Appendix 2 provides a detailed set of reminder checklists relating to necessary activities before, during and after the meeting. Part of this will involve identifying all the activities you need to undertake for each meeting you minute.

The focus of *this* chapter therefore, is to explore the *challenges* minute-takers face in the execution of the role and consider the actions which are necessary to overcome them, or at least minimise their impact. One of these challenges will be discussed in detail: the situation where the minute-taker is also required to take the notes *and* contribute at the same meeting.

The challenges of the minute-taking role

Although there will be some overlap, the problems experienced by minute-takers can be classified under two main headings:

- organisational; and
- personal.

Organisational problems are those caused by (a) the actions of individuals in the organisation (e.g. a poor chairperson or difficult participants) and (b) organisation culture, policies and practices (e.g. perception of low status or inadequate training). *Personal* problems are those which the minute-taker needs to address on a personal level (e.g. lack of confidence or poor listening skills).

Please read the following case study and then think about the organisational and personal issues which may have contributed to the less than successful outcome.

THE ROLE OF THE MINUTE-TAKER AND ITS CHALLENGES   13

> ### CASE STUDY
>
> Sarndeep was an inexperienced minute-taker. She had taken notes at several departmental team briefings, but never at a board meeting. Because of her willing and cooperative attitude she was asked to stand in for the regular minute-taker – who was otherwise engaged – at the next board meeting. The expectation in terms of the final minutes was for clearly presented decisions preceded by a reasonable level of background detail and discussion. Sarndeep was not given a pre-meeting briefing either by the regular minute-taker or by the chairperson. She was given a copy of the agenda and the minutes of the previous meeting, just prior to the meeting itself. She knew none of the board members by name and, except for the chairperson, none of them knew her. When she entered the meeting room, she was asked to sit in a chair which was placed some distance away from the chairperson. When the meeting commenced the chairperson mentioned to the group that Sarndeep was present for the purpose of taking the minutes but none of the members were invited to introduce themselves. Fortunately, just prior to the commencement of the meeting, Sarndeep had 'numbered' each of the participants as a form of identifier. As the meeting progressed there was much that Sarndeep didn't understand; for example, there was extensive use of jargon and technical terms. Nevertheless, she took the notes the best she could. At no point did she interrupt to seek clarifications and the chairperson did not summarise the key points and decisions at the end of each agenda item. Sarndeep left the room immediately following the conclusion of the meeting. When the draft minutes were circulated, extensive amendments were necessary. Even the finally circulated set was considered to be 'not up to the usual standard'.

Case analysis

What did you conclude? There are clearly a number of organisational issues that can be identified and a number of personal issues can possibly be inferred; indeed the blend of the two appears to have exacerbated the problem. Sarndeep was a willing but inexperienced minute-taker, asked to minute an important meeting; a meeting where the final minutes provide an evidential record for legal purposes. Surely, a pre-meeting briefing with either the regular minute-taker or the chairperson or both, should have been a pre-requisite? The agenda and minutes of the previous meeting were given to Sarndeep far too late; she had no time to clarify any points of concern either through background research or in face-to-face discussions with participants. Sarndeep was seated too far away from the chairperson; had she been closer it would have been easier to ask for clarifications and summaries. Clearly, the chairperson failed to appreciate the support an inexperienced minute-taker like Sarndeep would require and the 'delegation' of the task by the regular minute-taker appears to have been more of an abdication! This notwithstanding, was there more that Sarndeep herself could have done? Consider the following: Should she have *insisted* on a meeting with either the regular minute-taker or the chairperson? Could she have introduced herself to the participants prior to the start of the meeting and asked for their names? Should she have asked to be seated closer to the chairperson? Why did she not interrupt when she failed to understand the technically oriented parts of the discussion? At the very least, could she have asked the chairperson for a brief summary at the end of each agenda item? Why did she not approach the chairperson and/or the participants *after* the meeting to seek clarification?

Perhaps Sarndeep was a little lacking in self-confidence and found it difficult to be assertive. She may have been fearful of 'showing weakness'. If she was, why did she feel that way? Could some of this fear have been 'shaped' by the predominant corporate culture? Whatever the underlying reasons, the reality of the situation was that *she* failed to speak up and the *organisation* failed to provide the needed support.

In the scenario above, nobody wins. The chairperson (and possibly some of the participants) wastes valuable time in correcting the inaccurate draft. Sarndeep's self-confidence probably took a further knock and she will no doubt be quite reluctant to take on a similar task again.

Have you observed or experienced similar scenarios in your organisation? All minute-takers will struggle with a range of personal and organisational problems to a lesser or greater degree. Before thinking about how to negotiate them, the first stage is to *identify* them.

> ### STOP AND THINK
>
> Using a piece of notepaper, please take a few minutes to complete the following exercise:
>
> (a) Think carefully about the minute-taking activity in your organisation. From your experience and/or observation, make a list of all the *organisational* issues and problems you can think of which have a negative impact on the minute-taking process.
>
> (b) Think carefully about your experiences as a minute-taker. Make a list of all the *personal* issues and problems you can think of which have a negative impact on your own minute-taking effectiveness.

How long were your lists? Where did you find the greater concentration of problems – in the organisational category or the personal area? The more important question of course is: how can these problems be successfully negotiated? The following tables identify some of the more common problems in each category and provide suggestions for addressing them.

Table 2.1: Organisational issues

Organisational issues	Recommended action
Perception: low status function	Build credibility. Interact with participants before and after the meeting. Be assertive. Demonstrate that you are a fellow professional.
Perception: 'anyone can do it'	Actions speak louder than words here. Be professional in fulfilling every aspect of your role. If people think it's an easy task because you make it look easy, so what? They'll soon notice a difference if one day you're not there!

Table 2.1: *continued*

Organisational issues	Recommended action
No provision of training	Take the initiative here. There may be opportunities for informal training by approaching experienced colleagues and asking for assistance. Arrange to attend a formal minute-taking course; ideally ask for this to be built in to your personal appraisal-driven objectives.
Procrastination by participants	You will not eliminate this entirely. However, aim to provide periodic reminders to both the chairperson and the participants that the deadlines built in to the meeting cycle need to be adhered to; this is in everyone's interests.
Unclear contributions from participants	Interrupt and seek clarification from the contributor and/or ask the chairperson to clarify.
Demands from 'forceful' participants	On occasion, a participant may demand inclusion of certain comments in the minutes (or strongly assert that certain comments should *not* be included). You may not agree with this. In such cases, tactfully remind the person that you will follow the agreed minute-taking standards and that the chairperson will make any necessary amendments before presenting them for approval at the next meeting.
Asked to perform ancillary activities	Your professional performance will suffer if you are expected to undertake needless additional tasks during the meeting. Although the ordering of refreshments etc. may form part of the *pre-meeting* administration; let it be known that you are not there to pour the coffee!
Ineffective chairperson	An effectively chaired meeting is pivotal to its success. The negative impact of organisational issues is reduced when the chairperson is effective. Unfortunately, the converse is true. Be courageous; raise any concerns with the chairperson directly!
Decisions and actions unclear	Interrupt the chairperson and ask for clarification. Ask the chairperson to summarise at the end of each agenda item.
'Rambling' meetings	Meetings that are continually allowed to veer off-track will not be effective. Encourage the chairperson to establish clear objectives for each agenda item.
Excessive AOB section	Remind the chairperson of the true purpose of AOB and suggest that adjustments be made to current practice.
Unsuitable venue	An unsuitable venue (e.g. too small, poorly ventilated, inadequate facilities, noisy etc.) will affect the quality of the meeting and your ability to concentrate. Speak to the chair and explain the benefits of choosing an appropriate environment.

Table 2.1: *continued*

Organisational issues	Recommended action
'Falsification' of the minutes by the chair	Real falsification is rare. The chairperson has the right to make amendments, but if you are asked to do anything which makes you feel uncomfortable, discuss your concerns openly and frankly; it is important that you maintain your personal and professional integrity.
Expectation: every word to be recorded	This is neither practical nor beneficial. If necessary, explain to participants the clear benefits of concise summaries and the negative aspects of a verbatim record.
'Fussy' amendments following the draft	Do not give in to the whims of participants. Explain clearly that there is a set process for the approval of minutes and that this process must be adhered to.
Unreasonable timescales	Explain clearly how the existing timescale for production of the minutes is linked to the meeting cycle and that 'short-cuts' may compromise the quality and accuracy of the minutes.
Excessively long meetings	Overly long meetings sap the energy levels of everyone, so tend to lose their value past a certain point. Encourage the chairperson to allocate set timings for each agenda item.
Unsupportive culture	Sometimes you have to 'fight for your rights'! Be assertive. Ensure that you have all you need to carry out your role effectively.
Frequent criticism	If you are an inexperienced minute-taker, mistakes may be drawn to your attention more frequently than you would like. Often this comes in the form of *criticism* rather than *critique*. Don't overly worry about *how* something is said; rather evaluate if what has been said is true. If it is, then make the necessary adjustments. Over time, these criticisms will diminish.
Lack of appreciation	Don't worry too much if people aren't 'patting you on the back' for a job well done. If they say nothing, at least they aren't complaining!

Table 2.2: Personal issues

Personal issues	Recommended action
Lack of knowledge about meeting topics	Prepare as much as possible prior to the meeting. Read background material and the previous minutes. If necessary, carry out additional research. Talk to the chairperson and the meeting participants.
Lack of knowledge about technical terms	Apply the same points as above. Then ensure that you maintain a written record of the terms and their meanings. Update and amend as necessary.

Table 2.2: *continued*

Personal issues	Recommended action
Lack of minute-taking experience	This can only be built over time. Therefore, take every opportunity to take minutes at meetings. As your experience grows, so will your confidence.
Unskilled as a minute-taker	If you are a new minute-taker, take the initiative to actively develop your skills in all aspects of the minute-taking role. Create your own personal development plan and stick to it.
Too many meetings to minute	If you really are being overloaded, then be assertive and explain clearly that quality may suffer if you continue with the same schedule. However, this feeling could also be a perception due to poor minute-taking techniques which result in more time being spent on the process than is necessary. If the latter is true take action to develop your skills and eliminate ineffective practice.
Inability to concentrate	You will naturally have some lapses in concentration over the course of a long meeting. If the problem persists, reassess your approach; you may be trying to write down too much which will make you tired. You can also lose concentration if you don't understand something. Don't be afraid to interrupt!
Difficulty in listening	This is always a challenge, but is one of the key skills for minute-takers. Again, writing too much impedes active listening. Writing less will enable you to listen more and focus on the key message.
Tendency to write down everything	This is a tendency for new and inexperienced minute-takers, but can still be a problem for those who have taken notes at meetings over many years. Learn to focus on the key points and use short phrases not sentences.
Frightened to make a mistake	Don't be! Everyone makes mistakes including the chairperson and the participants! Obviously you want to avoid pure carelessness, but look at genuine mistakes in a positive way; they provide a platform for development.
Chairperson difficult to approach	Take steps to develop the relationship. Show that you understand the challenges that the chairperson faces and aim to be supportive. When you need the chairperson to act on your behalf, be polite but specific and assertive when communicating your needs.
Participants difficult to approach	Don't be put off by personality traits when you need participants to provide you with information. Be clear in stating the reason for your request and be assertive. Express appreciation for their assistance.
Frightened to speak up during the meeting	Apprehension is natural, particularly if you are new to minute-taking. However, you will become more stressed if you fail to speak up when you don't understand, so take the plunge!

Table 2.2: *continued*

Personal issues	Recommended action
Lacking in confidence	If you struggle with self-confidence issues, the interpersonal aspects of the minute-taking process can be a struggle. However, the more proficient you become in the role, the more confident you will begin to feel. So, keep working hard at developing your skills set.
Frequent fatigue	Minute-taking involves intense mental activity. Manage your 'personal minute-taking environment'. Ensure you have all the necessary tools, sit correctly at the table to reduce strain on your back and writing arm and keep hydrated.
Poor summarising skills	Summarising is the key to effective note-taking and to writing up the final minutes. This takes practice. Aim to isolate the key points and decisions. To achieve this, listen more and write less.
Difficulty in composing the minutes	Again, this takes practice. Study examples of minutes and aim to develop your vocabulary. Keep a written record of useful words and phrases for reference.
Difficulties in completing the draft on time	If you are new or inexperienced, you may spend a long time trying to produce the 'perfect' set of minutes. Producing the draft will become easier as your experience grows. If you are an *experienced* minute-taker and are still struggling with this area, you probably need to book yourself on a time management course!
Worried about what other people think	This is a fruitless trait. You cannot control the thoughts of others. Just be professional and those thoughts are likely to be positive.
Difficulty in taking notes and contributing	Don't just stumble on, hoping for the best here. You need to develop a clear strategy (see tips further on in the chapter).
Feeling stressed	Apply all the points above!

Think for a moment about the recommended actions described in the tables above. If a minute-taker were to apply all those recommended actions what do you think the result would be? Well it would be unrealistic to expect all the problems to just disappear but, over time, many of them would significantly diminish. How *easy* would it be to apply those actions? Look at the box and note some of the words and phrases that were used in the descriptions. Do you see a common theme emerging? Yes, the effective minute-taker must be proactive. This theme recurs throughout the book, like a melody in a song. This quality is vital because it allows the minute-taker to take control and embrace the challenges, rather than be overwhelmed by them. Choosing to take a proactive stance may be an attitude of mind, but it requires the application of a range of personal qualities. Chapter 13 addresses these areas in detail.

The dual role: taking notes and contributing in the same meeting

No matter how good you may be at multi-tasking, being both minute-taker and a participant in the same meeting will present challenges. That said, there are advantages and disadvantages to this type of arrangement. These are summarised below.

Table 2.3: Advantages and disadvantages of multi-tasking

Advantages	Disadvantages
• Greater knowledge of the subject matter • Greater familiarity with the chairperson and other participants • Increased status in the eyes of the participants • Easier to be assertive	• Hard to speak and record at the same time • Difficulties are increased when the chairperson is not effective • Difficulty in regaining concentration after making a contribution • Danger of emotions introducing bias

So, on the one hand, you are likely to be more confident, have a greater awareness of the issues being discussed and enjoy equal status in the eyes of the other participants. On the other hand, you are faced with an uphill struggle when you try to speak and record at the same time and regaining focus on note-taking can be difficult after making a contribution (particularly if it is lengthy). Also, you are likely to hold strong opinions on some topics and there is a risk that your strength of feeling could affect the objectivity of the final minutes. However, there *are* strategies that you can adopt to effectively meet this challenge:

- If you have become actively immersed in the discussions, Interrupt as and when necessary to seek clarification; particularly in relation to the key points of the discussion.
- Together with the group, create agreed standards regarding the level of detail to be included in the final minutes.
- Ask the chairperson to summarise elements of the discussion in a systematic way, particularly the decisions and actions.
- If your contribution is regularly limited to perhaps one or two items, you could consider passing the note-taking task to another member of the group for these items only. If you do adopt this strategy, please remember to provide at least a basic level of note-taking training!
- Be conscious of the need to maintain objectivity. It may be helpful to invite another member of the group to read over your initial draft with this requirement in mind and provide feedback.
- Following a particularly lengthy or emotionally-charged contribution, ask for a brief moment to re-focus before resuming note-taking activity. If no one has been taking the notes for you, this might be an appropriate point to discuss and agree with the group, the key points to be included in the minutes.

Summary

This chapter has emphasised some of the organisational and personal challenges that the minute-taker is likely to face. In functional terms, the role of the minute-taker involves undertaking a range of activities before, during and after the meeting. However, it is the organisational and personal problems inherent in those activities which are likely to induce the greater stress level, not necessarily the activities themselves. Suggestions were provided to help minute-takers address these problems and the overriding message was clear: to be successful in negotiating these challenges, minute-takers must be proactive. So, whether you are a new recruit or an 'old-hand', the challenges of minute-taking will be ever-present. You can have full confidence in meeting these challenges if you take ownership of the role and stay proactive!

Of course many of the organisational challenges derive from the meeting itself; how it is structured and conducted. It is likely that you will be required to take notes at more than one type of meeting and some of the challenges you may experience are likely to vary accordingly. So, what different types of meetings are there and what challenges do they pose for you as the minute-taker? These questions will be addressed in Chapter 3.

3
Meetings: types, purpose and structure

It's probably fair to say that if you were to ask just about anyone employed in an organisation to reveal their number one pet hate about organisational life, attending meetings would feature prominently in the replies!

Each and every day, all over the world, holding meetings is part and parcel of organisational life. Effective meetings contribute towards the successful implementation of an organisation's strategy but, far too often, meetings fail to achieve their purpose resulting in frustration for all involved. Poorly conducted meetings will make your minute-taking task even more challenging, so it is important to be aware of best practice principles; if you are proactive this will enable you to make suggestions to the chairperson for improvement where necessary. Also, if you are a contributor you can reflect on your own performance!

This chapter provides a brief overview of some of the different types of meeting you may be called upon to minute. It then considers why meetings fail and ways to make them more effective. A typical structure for a meeting is then presented, together with a brief explanation of some of the terminology applicable to more formal meetings.

Types of meeting

Types of meetings will naturally vary between different organisations. For example, student liaison meetings would be a regular feature in the calendar of a university, but not that of a car manufacturer! Notwithstanding these differences, there are meetings which are common to many organisations. Some of these are highlighted below:

Annual General Meeting (AGM)

A formal meeting, held annually, where, in the case of a company, those responsible for running it (the directors) meet with those who own it (the shareholders). The AGM for a public limited company (Plc) must be held annually and can be quite a high-profile affair. These meetings may be open to media scrutiny and require a lot of careful thought and planning. For private limited companies, the articles may stipulate that an AGM should be held, but there is no longer a statutory requirement to do so (Companies Act 2006). Similarly, with regard to charities, the AGM provides an opportunity for the members to meet with those running the charity (trustees and/or officers) to ask questions about the management of the charity prior to voting. The governing document will state whether an AGM is required. The articles will stipulate whether an AGM is required for charitable companies.

Minutes should be taken at an AGM. In terms of style and format, you should check the requirements regarding layout and level of detail. It is helpful to study examples from previous years, particularly if you're taking the minutes of an AGM for the first time. Usually the style will be succinct and formal.

Extraordinary General Meeting (EGM)

This is a general meeting which is called to deal with urgent matters which require resolution between AGMs. (For companies formed under the Companies Act 2006, the word: 'extraordinary' has now been dropped.) The same principles apply with regard to minute taking.

Board meetings

The directors of a company are responsible for managing its business on a day-to-day basis. As noted in Chapter 1, it is important that directors are not negligent in the execution of their duties and the minutes of board meetings provide evidence of the decisions taken. According to ICSA's *Code of Good Boardroom Practice*, the minutes should record the decisions taken and provide sufficient background to those decisions. Therefore, the minutes of board meetings will be lengthier than the minutes of general meetings, but they should still be concise and provide a clear summary of the decisions taken. Of course, this type of meeting is not just limited to companies. Meetings of this nature are held across a wide variety of organisations and the minute-taking principles highlighted here will be broadly applicable.

Local authority meetings

With regard to the transaction of local authority business, individual authorities will have their own preferences regarding the form that the minutes should take. However, the emphasis should be on a clear and concise recording of the decisions taken and the reasons for taking them. The formality of council proceedings tends to be reflected in the style of council minutes. The style may be different for *committee* minutes, but the same emphasis on precision and clarity will apply. There are of course other types of public services, for example, NHS boards and specific preferences regarding form and style will also apply here.

Committee meetings

These are meetings involving groups that are set up to support the work of the Board. There are many different types of committees within organisations and requirements in terms of the minutes will vary. The general principles of clarity and brevity will usually apply, although some committees (e.g. joint consultative committees) may require a greater level of background detail.

Management meetings

Management meetings can take many forms depending on the structure of the organisation. These meetings involve managerial decision making at various levels. For example, some meetings will involve the senior management team, while others will involve middle management or will cover both groups. The general principles for effective minute-taking apply; the style and format will be based on established practice and the preferences of the group.

Conferences and 'away-days'

Where organisations hold management conferences, it is usual to make a record of the main proceedings. The exact format for this will depend on organisational requirements and preferences. At some conferences, parallel workshops are also conducted. These are mini break-out sessions and usually involve a presentation on a particular topic, perhaps delivered by someone external to the organisation. There may be a requirement for the main points from these sessions to be noted. Alternatively, papers may have been circulated by the presenter and these can be attached to a summary of the main proceedings.

Departmental meetings

These are periodic or one-off meetings attended by all departmental staff to discuss and address departmental issues (e.g. reviewing performance, setting objectives, reporting on the outcome of actions taken and discussing any other matters in connection with departmental operations). It is usual to take minutes at such meetings.

Steering group meetings

A steering group may be formed to take a high-level overview of a project. The group is usually composed of senior executives, project leaders and possibly external advisors to the organisation. Minutes should be kept of steering group meetings.

Project team meetings

Project teams may be formed for all manner of reasons. In a large organisation there may be many different projects being carried out at the same time. Large projects, such as the implementation of a new IT system, would necessarily involve the establishment of sub-groups to handle different aspects of the project. In a change management programme for example, one team may be formed to deal with the human resources aspects of organisational change, while another deals with organisational structure and work process changes, with yet another for the development of new IT infrastructures. It is important that minutes are taken at project review meetings which clearly highlight the salient issues, the key decisions and the agreed actions.

Team briefings

These are meetings held by the team leader to discuss issues with members of the team (e.g. progress reviews, allocation of tasks, setting objectives, performance and motivational issues). A full set of formal minutes is not really required in such a meeting as the emphasis is likely to be more on actions and who will take them. Therefore, a set of notes detailing the key actions to be taken and those responsible for them will probably suffice.

One-off informal meetings

These can take place anywhere at any time. They may be informal discussions between one or two employees or a small group. It would be very unusual for any notes to be taken at gatherings like this, but this does not mean that such meetings carry no value; some of the most creative ideas are often generated over a cup of coffee!

Effective and ineffective meetings

> **STOP AND THINK**
>
> Please take a few minutes to think about the following two questions and then jot down your answers on a piece of paper:
>
> (a) Think carefully about the meetings you have attended over the course of your professional life. Focus on those that either failed or were ineffective. In your opinion, what were the factors which made these meetings ineffective?
> (b) Now think carefully about those meetings that worked well. What factors do you think contributed to their success?

Did you find it easier to identify the *ineffective* meetings? Don't worry if you did; it seems that in many organisations, really effective meetings are the exception rather than the rule. Even where meetings are conducted reasonably well, there are often areas for improvement, so a periodic evaluation of meeting effectiveness is always a good idea. The following table summarises some of the factors which make a meeting either effective or ineffective.

Table 3.1: Factors which make a meeting effective or ineffective

Effective meetings	Ineffective meetings
• Clear purpose and objectives • Clear link to organisational strategy • Good level of preparation by all • All necessary paperwork to hand • Strong chairperson/minute-taker relationship • Clear decisions, no ambiguity, consensus • Clearly defined actions • Willingness to take responsibility for actions • Active participation • Freedom to express views • Active listening by all participants • Contributions from all members encouraged • Assertively chaired • No 'hidden agendas' • No political manoeuvring • Well-structured agenda • Logical development of agenda items • Correct use of AOB or no AOB • Meeting not overly long • Punctual start • Timed agenda items • Timings adhered to for each item • Meeting concluded on time • Suitable venue • Reliable equipment	• Held when not required • Held too frequently • Not held frequently enough • Held simply as a matter of routine • Poorly defined purpose • Lack of clear objectives • Lack of preparation • Key participants missing • Wrong people invited • Unclear decisions and actions • Autocratic chairperson • Passive chairperson • Poor participation from some members • Strong personalities allowed to dominate • Irrelevant discussion • Aggressive contributions tolerated • Disruptive behaviour tolerated • Poorly-structured agenda • Misuse of AOB • Excessively long • No timings on agenda items • Poor punctuality • Unsuitable venue • Hidden agendas • Political manoeuvring

As a minute-taker, it is in your interests to exert whatever influence you can so that the meetings you attend are characterised by points in the effective list above. In this regard, much can be achieved if your relationship with the chairperson is strong. It is unrealistic to expect that every meeting will exhibit these characteristics all the time and many factors will be outside your control. Nevertheless, you are strongly encouraged to keep 'chipping away': much can be gained by remaining proactive! You also need to lead by example. You can do this in two ways. First, many of the activities within your minute-taking role will affect the quality of the meeting so remain professional at all times. Second, it is likely that minute-taking is only part of your job role. You may attend some meetings purely as a participant. It may be that you have managerial responsibility and are required to chair a number of meetings. Of course, at some meetings you may undertake the dual role of both minute-taker and participant. The following points are useful tips for promoting best practice as a participant.

- Always study and absorb all material that has been circulated prior to the meeting.
- Always arrive, for any meeting, in plenty of time and fully prepared.
- When you speak, always have something meaningful to say.
- Ensure your comments relate to the objectives of the specific item being discussed and also, that they dovetail with the overall objectives of the meeting.
- Never become embroiled in purely personal disagreements.
- Always be prepared to fully express your true feelings and viewpoint on the matters being discussed, but retain self-control.
- Take the trouble to investigate the cultural norms, preferences and expectations of the individual participants. Be culturally sensitive when making comments.
- Be prepared to yield on issues where there is no real point of principle involved.
- If you are making a presentation, consider the use of visual aids to enhance the delivery.
- If there is a designated break in the proceedings, always be back in your seat early, ready for a prompt re-start.
- Following the meeting, conduct a self-evaluation. Ask yourself: How well did I fulfil my role as a participant?
- If you are delegated the responsibility for a particular action, then follow up quickly and efficiently.
- Avoid being critical of the meeting outside the meeting room.
- Always respect confidentiality.

These next points will also be applicable if you hold managerial responsibility and are required to periodically organise and chair meetings (the role of the chairperson is discussed in detail in Chapter 4).

- If you hold a position of management responsibility, try to ensure your team are empowered in their job roles. This will create a spirit where meetings become opportunities for rich discussion.
- Periodically, review the quality of your meetings. If you have leadership responsibilities then conduct a full evaluation (i.e. written feedback from each participant) then review ways in which the process could be improved.
- Occasionally, sit back and analyse: What would happen if this meeting did not take place? The answer will either highlight its importance or its lack of usefulness.
- Be prepared to scrap routine meetings if they are serving no real purpose (i.e. where they do not meaningfully support the pursuance of company objectives).
- Calculate the cost of particular meetings and then evaluate if it is providing value for money.

Meeting structure

If a meeting is to be effective, it must have a clear sense of direction. A meeting without structure is likely to veer off-track and end up as more of a 'talking shop'. The structure will vary depending on the nature of the meeting and the level of formality or informality. For example, a team meeting which is convened to brainstorm some ideas on a particular issue before deciding on a course of action may appear relatively unstructured. However, the team leader will still follow an unwritten structure, for example, as follows:

MEETINGS: TYPES, PURPOSE AND STRUCTURE

- Explain the purpose of the session
- Facilitate the session
  - Ask for ideas from the group
  - Record the ideas on a flipchart
- Discuss the findings
- Seek consensus on the best course of action.

A regular team briefing may have a written structure in the form of a list of points for discussion. A departmental meeting may involve issuing a more formal agenda with a list of items for discussion. People tend to associate formal meetings with a clearly defined structure and indeed there are a number of specific sections which tend to be included in the structure for such meetings. A typical framework is shown in the table below. This framework will be re-visited in Chapter 10 where the structure and layout of the minutes is discussed.

EXAMPLE

The structure of a meeting

Introduction
- Welcome by the chairperson
- Minute taker notes the names and any changes
- Introduction not usually minuted unless it takes the form of a specific agenda item

Apologies for absence
- Create an accurate list of attendees on the day
  - **S**ubstituting
  - **N**ot arrived
  - **A**pologies
  - **P**resent
- Declarations of Interest

Minutes of the previous meeting
- To approve the minutes as an accurate record
- The only discussion should relate to: 'Are the minutes accurate?'
- Concentrate on errors of fact
- Minutes should have been read by members BEFORE THE MEETING
- The filed set of minutes should NOT be altered
- The chair to sign

Matters arising
- A quick progress review
- A confirmation that agreed actions have been completed
- An update from an item(s) in previous minutes

> **EXAMPLE continued**
>
> Information only
> - Not for discussion or debate
> - If need for major discussion, incorporate as part of a main agenda item
> - Papers should be circulated with the agenda
> - A written report can be attached to the minutes. Verbal reports can be minuted.
>
> Agenda Items
> - The key topics for discussion at the meeting
>
> Any Other Business
> - **D**efer to the next meeting
> - **R**eject it
> - **A**ccept as genuine AOB
> - **F**it into the agenda
> - **T**rash it?
>
> Date of Next Meeting
> - Confirm the date of the next meeting

The issue of formality

The generic structure above can be adapted to the requirements of the particular meeting. The order of items constitutes a logical flow but exact terminology may vary and not every section necessarily needs to be included in every meeting. Informal groups are unlikely to follow a structure such as this but, as previously noted, that doesn't mean that a structure is *not* followed even if it is unwritten. Indeed it is very important that relatively informal meetings, such as team briefings, have a clear direction; they are no less important to the operations of the organisation than the more formal meetings.

The rules applicable to formal meetings (e.g. general meetings and board meetings) are usually laid down in an organisation's governing document; in the case of a company, this would be the memorandum and articles of association. For example, a meeting is said to be *quorate* when the minimum number of directors entitled to vote are present. The quorum is usually fixed by the articles. If this is not the case then the common law rule applies (i.e. a quorum is two directors if not otherwise defined). Also, statutory rules in connection with meetings are contained in the Companies Act 2006. The principal statutory rules in respect of local authority meetings are contained in the Local Government Act 1972 and the Local Government and Housing Act 1989, Part I and various other enactments.

It is also important that the purpose and objectives of committees and sub-committees are clearly understood. Details regarding a committee's membership, the scope of its duties and the extent of its powers should be clearly defined in the *terms of reference* document.

As a minute-taker it is important that you are familiar with the rules governing each of the meetings you minute. For example, in a board meeting, the meeting must be quorate for *each* item of business. The minute-taker (in conjunction with the chair) needs to keep a check that a quorum exists.

As mentioned in the introductory chapter, it is not the purpose of this book to discuss in-depth the law and procedure of meetings, nor to provide detailed explanations of formal voting procedures. At board meetings it is quite rare for a formal vote to be taken, with decisions often arrived at by consensus. The following is a glossary of terms relating to the conducting of formal meetings.

Table 3.2: Glossary of meeting terms

Meeting term	Explanation
Abstention	Voting neither in favour nor against a motion
Ad hoc	'For this purpose'. For a specific purpose. A committee established temporarily for a special purpose
Adjournment	The postponement or suspension of a meeting
Agenda	The document indicating what is to be discussed at the meeting; the list of items presented in a logical order
Amendment	Alteration to a motion
Any other business	An item on the agenda which allows matters to be discussed which were not put on the agenda in advance. These should relate to important and/or urgent issues that would have been included on the agenda had they been known about at the time
Apologies	When a member of the group is unable to attend the meeting, they should send apologies for absence in advance of the meeting
Articles of Association	A document setting out regulations for a company's operations and defining how tasks are to be carried out
Casting vote	If the governing document allows: a second vote cast by the chairperson when votes are tied to produce a clear decision
Consensus	General agreement regarding the decisions taken
Ex-officio	The right to attend a meeting 'by virtue of one's office'
Matters arising	Discussion on questions and issues arising from the previous meeting
Memorandum of Association	A document required to incorporate a company, giving details such as the company name and names of subscribers
Motion	The name used when a proposal is being discussed at a meeting
Mover	A member speaking on behalf of a motion
Nem con	Latin: *nemine contradicente*; 'with no one contradicting' (possibly one or more abstentions)

Table 3.2: *continued*

Meeting term	Explanation
No confidence	A vote of 'no confidence' in the chairperson (due to disagreement with the chairperson e.g. biased rulings)
Point of order	A query regarding the procedure at a meeting. A member may perceive a breach of the agreed rules and raises a 'point of order'
Poll	A counted vote
Procedural motion	A motion relating to how the meeting is conducted (i.e. meeting procedures)
Proposal	An item submitted for discussion at a meeting
Proxy	A person who acts at a meeting on behalf of another person
Quorum	The minimum number of members who must be present to constitute a valid meeting
Resolution	A motion which has been carried at a meeting (after the formal decision has been reached)
Seconder	A member supporting the proposer of a motion by putting their name to it
Standing orders	Additional rules governing a group in the conducting of its business and meetings
Sub-committee	A sub-group appointed by a committee to handle part of its work
Substantive motion	A motion for debate (i.e. relating to the purpose of the meeting (often in an amended form))
Tabled	The introduction of a paper at the meeting (i.e. first seen at the meeting)
Terms of reference	A document setting out rules for a sub-group (what it can and cannot do; guidance for conducting its business etc)
Unanimous	When all members vote the same way (for or against)

Summary

This chapter has described the different types of meetings that are held within organisations and some of the expectations at such meetings with regard to the minutes. Some points regarding the effectiveness of meetings were also discussed and a typical structure for a formal meeting was highlighted. The chapter concluded with a brief consideration of the issue of formality, including voting procedures and the commonly used terms in connection with formal meetings.

Of course one of the key determinants of a successful meeting is the effectiveness of the chairperson. This vital role is discussed in detail in Chapter 4.

4
Understanding the role of the chairperson

Meetings would be so easy to minute if it wasn't for the chairperson and the participants! Such a sentiment is no doubt 'locked into the heart' of many a minute taker; even if they do not voice it publicly. Interestingly, in discussions with delegates on the Effective Minute-Taking course, issues with the chairperson appear as a recurring theme. The following issues are typical of the views expressed:

- Managing the minute-taking process where the chair is not particularly decisive
- Coping with a weak and ineffective chair
- Failure to summarise the key points and decisions
- Coping with the preferences of different chairpersons
- Ensuring that the chair brings any discussion to an identifiable decision
- Dealing with a passive chairperson
- Managing the chairperson's expectation for 'excellent quality' minutes within existing time constraints.

The effectiveness of the chairperson (or otherwise) is a critical factor in determining the effectiveness of the meeting and, by extension, the effectiveness of the minute-taking process. Minute-takers need some understanding of how the duties of a chairperson *should* be exercised. Armed with this knowledge, they will be in a better position to take a more proactive stance in managing the minute-taker/chairperson relationship.

The beginning of this chapter provides an overview of the role of the chairperson, highlighting the fundamental objectives. The role is then examined in greater detail, structured around checklists for three separate phases of activity: *careful planning* (before the meeting), *capability* (during the meeting) and *critical evaluation* (after the meeting).

Overview of the role

Essentially, the role of the chairperson is that of a leader. A good leader works towards a clearly defined set of goals and inspires others to follow in pursuance of those goals. Although an element of control may be exercised, this is done with a view to maximising the collective contribution from team members; in essence, a good leader achieves goals through people.

In any meeting, the principal goal is to arrive at a number of key decisions on a specified number of agenda items and to ensure that these decisions are recorded. These decisions are reached either through consensus or by majority vote, following a period of discussion. As leader, the chairperson is responsible for achieving this goal through people: the meeting participants. In order to do so, the chairperson must keep a tight focus on the meeting's objectives and manage it in an orderly fashion. Discussion on each agenda item must be sufficiently *long* to allow for the presentation of background and context and the airing of all the varying perspectives but sufficiently *short* to ensure that the discussion remains focused and 'on-track'. For a meeting to be effective, all discussions should take place in a professional manner, not be overly argumentative in nature and embrace the contributions of *all* the participants. The role of the chairperson then could be summarised as follows:

> To orchestrate the meeting in a way which maximises the constructive contribution from all participants and ensures that appropriate decisions are made, understood and recorded in respect of each agenda item, all within the designated timeframe for the meeting.

The above description may sound reasonably straightforward, but achieving it requires considerable skill! The chairperson must be a good planner, organiser, motivator, delegator and time manager. Personal qualities are also important. The chairperson should be an excellent communicator, assertive, enthusiastic, a good listener and emotionally intelligent. This may seem like quite a tall order and possibly explains why a problem with the chairperson remains a recurring theme with minute-takers!

The effective chairperson

In this section, the role of the chairperson is broken down into checklists of essential activities and skills under the three headings: *careful planning* (before the meeting), *capability* (during the meeting) and *critical evaluation* (after the meeting). Although these three headings are designed to present a broadly chronological structure to the review, there is a natural overlapping of activities and skills (e.g. some of the skills required *during the meeting* will have been developed prior to the meeting, indeed the development may be ongoing; also, some of them will be applicable to parts of the planning process and vice versa).

Careful planning

- *Understand the nature, purpose and objectives of the meeting*. A captain of a ship cannot chart a course successfully without knowing the destination! The chairperson needs to know exactly why the meeting has been called and its overall purpose. It is then easier to keep the meeting on course. This includes knowing the objectives of each agenda item and the areas where decisions are required.
- *Share the above information with the minute taker*. If the minute taker is aware of the key decision points, it will be easier to note and record them.

- *Create the agenda for the meeting*. The items should be grouped in a logical sequence; it may be beneficial to place the 'meatier' items for early discussion, while minds are still relatively fresh. The objectives for each item should be included together with the time allocation.
- *Provide timely information for participants*. With regard to accompanying papers and supporting information, it is important that the chair and the minute taker work together to ensure that meeting participants receive sufficient information about the decisions required – in good time.
- *Select and invite the participants*. For many meetings, the participant list may be pre-determined, but consideration needs to be given to any additional attendees that may be required and/or observers. For some meetings, there may be more freedom in selecting who attends. Where this is the case, the right 'mix' of people should be selected relative to the achievement of the meeting's objectives. Invitees should be fully informed of what is expected of them.
- *Meet with the minute-taker*. Communication with the minute-taker may take place on several occasions during the meeting preparation phase, but there should always be a short (five-minute) briefing just prior to commencement, to ensure that the objectives are fully understood and that all is in order.
- *Research the key topic areas*. Although the chairperson does not need to be the 'expert' on every issue being discussed, they should be conversant with the key themes, objectives and areas of possible contention. Research prior to the meeting is recommended.
- *Be aware of the varying perspectives of the participants*. Each participant comes to the meeting with particular views, opinions and objectives. Within reason, the chairperson needs to be aware of these because they will feed into the discussions. It is helpful to know beforehand any areas of possible contention, vested interests and likely political manoeuvring. This could be achieved – at least in part – by researching the historical backdrop surrounding the item being placed on the agenda and by speaking to the participants individually, prior to the meeting.
- *Know the personalities of the participants*. During the meeting itself, the chairperson will need to ensure that a balanced contribution is achieved from the participant body. Prior awareness of personality types could be beneficial here when planning how to manage the discussions (drawing out the reserved and controlling the verbose).
- *Know the strengths and weaknesses of the participants*. When actions are required following on from decisions taken at the meeting, prior knowledge of participants' strengths and weaknesses can assist in the allocation of responsibilities.
- *Take steps to manage potential hostility*. Although a healthy level of debate and discussion of alternate points of view can be a positive thing in arriving at decisions, if, prior to the meeting, it becomes apparent that outright hostility exists which threatens the successful outcome of the meeting, then the chairperson may need to take steps to reduce or eliminate that hostility prior to commencement. This could happen by investigating the root cause of the problem and speaking directly with the individual(s) concerned with the aim of reaching a workable solution.
- *Speak with participants prior to the meeting*. This may happen just prior to the meeting or sometime before. If the latter, this will provide the opportunity to build enthusiasm for the meeting and foster a collaborative spirit. At the meeting itself, the chairperson should be a welcoming host. Being on hand to greet participants and build rapport can do much to diffuse any anxiety (particularly if new invitees are present) and create a more relaxed atmosphere prior to the meeting.

- *Oversee the necessary administrative arrangements.* Although the mechanics of this will likely be delegated, the chairperson should ensure that the arrangements are carried out effectively.

Capability

- *Be punctual.* The meeting should always begin on time. This sets the right psychological tone for all that is to follow, underscoring the importance of the proceedings and adding to the chairperson's credibility.
- *Introduce the meeting in a welcoming yet professional manner.* Setting the right tone for the meeting is important. Everyone should be warmly welcomed to the meeting and appropriate introductions should be made, particularly if new attendees are present. The chairperson should state the purpose of the meeting and provide a brief overview of the agenda before leading into the first item.
- *Remember participants' names.* This reinforces the professionalism of the chairperson and helps to maintain a collaborative atmosphere. For some meetings, remembering names will not be a problem, but for others, this may pose more of a challenge. Depending on the nature of the meeting, the use of name cards might be a good idea. Another technique is to record the names on a piece of paper and place it near the agenda.
- *Cover the opening items of the meeting reasonably quickly.* 'Apologies for absence', 'Minutes of the last meeting', and 'Matters arising from the minutes', should be fairly 'standard' items which can be dealt with quickly. Although brief updates may be required under 'Matters arising', this section should not be allowed to swallow up too much of the time allocated for the meeting as a whole; the agenda items that follow are the 'core' of the meeting and the majority of the time should be allocated to these.
- *Explain the purpose of each of the main agenda items.* The chairperson should open the discussion on each of the agenda items, with an overview of its purpose and the prime objectives. This will help to focus minds and make it easier for the chairperson to justifiably 'rein-in' discussion when it veers off-point. It's also really useful for the minute-taker!
- *Ensure that the discussion is correctly time-managed.* There are four elements to this: First, the chairperson must ensure that discussion on *all* items is concluded within the overall time allocated for the meeting. Second, the time allocated for each individual item should be strictly observed. Third, the discussion on each item should be carefully time-managed to ensure a balanced contribution on the key points (allowing for any pre-determined weighting factors). Finally, participants' individual contributions should be time-managed to ensure a balanced contribution is achieved overall.
- *Keep the discussion 'on-track'.* The discussion on each agenda item is shaped by the pre-set objectives for that item. The chairperson must ensure that the discussion doesn't lose its shape by a tendency to dwell on irrelevancies. Any valid issues which may emerge from the discussions – but which are not directly related to the objectives – should be noted and placed on a subsequent agenda.
- *Encourage everyone to actively participate.* This is one of the biggest challenges for any chairperson! In theory at least, everyone eligible to participate at the meeting (some will be members of the group, others will be there to advise and others may be simply observers) has

something meaningful to contribute or they wouldn't be there. However, the diverse range of personalities on show can pose difficulties: some are quiet and reserved, others are loud and proud! Some struggle to make a point out of fear of rejection, others seem to enjoy raising controversial points and kick-starting arguments. The following table highlights some typical personality types and provides some tips on how the chairperson can manage them.

Table 4.1: Different personality types

Personality type	Characteristics	Chair's strategy
The talker	These people love the sound of their own voice. Their contributions are valid, but because they *always* have something to say, valuable time may be 'hijacked' from other contributors.	Time-manage their specific contributions. You may need to interrupt in an assertive way, sum-up the point and move on. 'Ration' the number of times they contribute on a given topic and actively invite others in.
The expert	The know-alls who like everyone to know they know! Their contributions may be valuable, but they may not know as much as they think they know on every topic.	Praise contributions but, if necessary, regulate the frequency of input. Use pointed questions to make them justify their assertions. Others may feel inferior and hold back, so actively bring others in when you know they have a valid – and perhaps alternative – point of view.
The waffler	People who say in 50 words what could be said in 10! They may be harmless and actually have a meaningful point to make, but it is often obscured by the overly wordy expressions used.	Listen carefully to extract the main point from the contribution, then summarise it and ask back to check understanding (e.g. 'So, your key point of concern is....?').Then restate it for the benefit of the other participants.
The aggressor	The verbal bullies. If they do not get their own way, they may forcefully and aggressively criticise the contributions of others who hold an alternative point of view. Their behaviour may intimidate.	Whilst acknowledging any valid concerns, consistently assertive behaviour is required here. Ask them to justify their strong views and explain clearly why they disagree with any alternative viewpoints. Keep the objectives to the fore. Private but frank discussion outside the meeting (before or after) may be required if the aggressive stance persists.
The dormouse	Timid, shy or lacking in confidence. However, they are at the meeting for a reason and their contribution needs to be drawn out.	Use of specific questions can help here, along with gentle encouragement. Tactfully feeding the odd word or phrase to help them complete their expressions can help. Commend and praise.

Table 4.1: *continued*

Personality type	Characteristics	Chair's strategy
The wordsmith	Relatively harmless characters who have a valuable contribution to make, but who insist on making it using words and phrases that others find difficult to understand.	Talking to them before the meeting may help so that you know what the thrust of their argument will be, allowing you to summarise the main points in the meeting for everyone else!
The whisperer	This behaviour can be quite distracting and disconcerting. These participants frequently whisper to those seated on either side during the course of the meeting.	Be assertive. Only one person can talk at one time. This should be reinforced. Stop talking and see if you get a reaction, or pose a question to ask if there's a problem. If the problem persists it should be addressed directly with the individual outside the meeting.
The politician	They have hidden agendas and try to manipulate events based on those agendas. This may involve speaking with other participants prior to the meeting to garner support for a particular view, or seeking to play one person off against another. They can be dangerous if their agendas conflict with the meeting's objectives.	Knowledge of the participants is needed here. Speak with them and try to determine their motives. During the meeting it may be possible to overlook some of the tactical positioning, but if there appears to be a genuine threat to the achievement of the meeting's objectives, such tactics must be exposed and dealt with immediately.
The critic	Passive-aggressive behaviour, which may appear innocuous, but on closer inspection reveals a cynical and negative approach. There appears to be no genuine desire to find solutions or move things forward.	Initially, pointed questions can be used to make them justify their negative stance. If the situation persists, frank open one-to-one discussions may help to reveal the cause of the problem (e.g. some form of perceived injustice, or disillusionment with the decision-making process).

- *Employ effective questioning techniques.* Managing the discussion on each agenda item can be challenging and demanding. The effective use of questions is essential if the chairperson is to draw out all the relevant points leading to the key decisions. *Open* questions are necessary to get participants talking: 'How do you think the problem could be tackled?' or 'What factors need to be considered before we agree to proceed?' *Closed* questions can be used to check understanding: 'Is that point now fully clear?' or to seek agreement to proceed: 'Are we ready to move on?' *Rhetorical* questions can be used to good effect when the chairperson wishes to stimulate thinking just prior to making an important point. Throughout the discussion clarification will be required, elaboration on points will be necessary, greater depth of detail will need to be extracted and attitudes and views will need to be challenged. All this can be successfully managed through the effective use of questions.

- *Provide frequent summaries*. As the discussion progresses on an agenda item, one good way of maintaining focus is to summarise the key arguments and sections of discussion. This approach helps to crystallise thinking thus making it easier to reach the final decision(s). This technique is also helpful to the minute-taker, particularly where the item is long and the subject matter is detailed.
- *Use humour*. A meeting is not the place for a stand-up comedy routine! Nevertheless, appropriate use of humour can do a lot to ease tension and take the heat out of potentially explosive situations. The humour should be natural, not contrived and it should never embarrass or upset any of the participants.
- *Be patient*. Although it is necessary for the chairperson to take control and move the meeting along, not all speakers are fluent in expressing their ideas. Patience and tact is required here, to draw ideas out and assist the participant to grow in confidence.
- *Be enthusiastic*. Enthusiasm is infectious, but so is a lack of it! The chairperson should display appropriate enthusiasm before, during and after the meeting when interacting with participants, but it is particularly important during the meeting itself. An enthusiastic chairperson can do much to keep the spirit of the meeting alive and encourage participants to actively engage in the discussions.
- *Be assertive*. A passive chairperson frustrates participants and an aggressive one risks alienating them. An assertive chairperson respects the rights of others and encourages meaningful contributions, but is not afraid to take control, challenge attitudes or, where necessary, to deal emphatically with disruptive behaviour. A calm yet firm approach wins the respect of others.
- *Be conscious of body language*. Most research seems to conclude that, with regard to communication, people attach more significance to the *visual* message than the verbal. Therefore, the visual signals displayed by the chairperson should be congruent with the verbal message. The chairperson should maintain good eye contact with participants and also carefully observe *their* body language; much may be revealed about attitudes, opinions and strength of feeling even though no words are spoken.
- *Be an active listener*. Effective questioning techniques are not much good without effective listening techniques! The chairperson needs to listen carefully to contributions to understand the point being made and be in a position to ask the next question to move the discussion forward.
- *Speak at a comfortable volume*. The chairperson needs to hold the attention of the group. Speaking at too low a volume will 'lose' the audience and speaking too loudly will irritate them. In a large meeting room, it will be necessary to project the voice a little more than usual, but shouting must be avoided. Projection can be aided by keeping eye contact when addressing the group and by voice 'warm-up' practice (e.g. a few simple deep-breathing exercises, before the start of the meeting).
- *Dress appropriately*. The nature of the meeting will suggest what constitutes appropriate attire. The key point is that nothing should detract from the chairperson's role. The participants need to concentrate on what the chairperson is saying and not the degree of sartorial elegance … or lack of it!
- *Deal with tension and conflict*. Much can be done prior to the meeting to reduce potential conflict. Simply identifying the contentious issues and speaking to participants who hold strong views and acknowledging their strength of feeling can help to set the scene for a more

controlled debate. Notwithstanding this, discussions can and do become heated on occasions. The chairperson needs to set the example throughout the meeting regarding keeping tempers in check, avoiding personal attacks or displaying aggressive body language. When introducing items likely to cause conflict, the chairperson can acknowledge this and preface the discussion with an appeal for a level-headed debate. *Assertive* body language may help where disruption persists (e.g. *standing up* can be an effective display of the chairperson's authority) and can serve to bring the meeting to order. In some situations, taking a short break, or even deferring the item to another agreed time may help to diffuse tensions. If the meeting cannot be brought under control, ending it at that point may be the only option, but all other options should have been tried before this decision is made.

- *Summarise the decisions reached*. At the end of each agenda item, the chairperson should summarise the decisions taken. This is beneficial for the participants and certainly for the minute-taker!
- *Clearly identify the actions and the person(s) responsible*. Where actions arise from the decisions taken, the chairperson should ensure that everyone understands what these are, who is responsible for them and the agreed timescales for completion.
- *Conclude the meeting*. The meeting should always be concluded on a positive note, even if it has been characterised by heated debate and an element of conflict.
- *Conduct a brief review with the minute-taker*. This is to check that the minute-taker has all the required information in terms of background, decisions and actions. It is also an opportunity to build rapport and express appreciation for the vital role the minute-taker performs.

Critical evaluation

- *Critically evaluate the effectiveness of the meeting in detail*. An effective chairperson continually seeks to improve. Following the meeting, the chairperson should reflect on the points in the box below. If the reflection reveals areas requiring improvement, the chairperson should address these prior to the next meeting.
- *Check the draft minutes when produced*. This part of the process can often leave the minute-taker frustrated, particularly when the chairperson makes numerous corrections, none of which the minute-taker agrees with! However, the likelihood of tensions arising is minimised when the chairperson applies all the points featured in the *careful planning* and *capability* sections above. By doing so, the minute-taker will have been reminded of all the key decisions and actions during the meeting and given a chance to discuss any concerns and check understanding in the one-to-one meeting between minute-taker and chairperson. Also, the chairperson will have prepared for and conducted the meeting in a structured way, thus aiding retention in terms of the key points. There is, therefore, a greater chance that both parties will be 'singing from the same song sheet' as it were, thereby minimising the level of disagreement.
- *Assist the minute-taker to improve*. Notwithstanding the points made above, it may be that the minute-taker still requires some guidance in certain areas (e.g. there may be political sensitivities which affect the way sentences should be worded, or legal issues which impact on the phrases selected). The chairperson can work with the minute-taker on these points in the mutual interest.

- *Return the draft minutes.* The timeframe for this should be agreed between the minute-taker and the chairperson. Corrections can then be made by the minute-taker prior to circulation.
- *Begin preparation for the next meeting.* Having signed-off the minutes (for approval at the next meeting) the chairperson can begin preparing for the next meeting. This may include an element of progress-chasing and following up on actions, where these impact on and feed into the agenda for the following meeting.

CHECKLIST

Areas for reflection

Did I prepare thoroughly for the meeting? If I did, how did that impact on the effectiveness of the meeting? If I did not, how did that impact on the effectiveness of the meeting?

Did the meeting commence on time?

Did the meeting finish on time?

Did I adhere to the pre-set timings for each agenda item?

Did I explain the purpose of the meeting at the outset?

Did I highlight the objectives for each agenda item?

Did the discussion on each agenda item remain focused on the objectives or did it veer off-point?

Were all participants able to have their say?

Did I employ appropriate questioning techniques to draw out all the key points?

How effectively did I listen to the contributions made?

How effectively did I deal with the varying personalities within the group?

How well did I control the meeting?

Was there any disruptive behaviour or conflict? If so, how did I handle it?

On the longer agenda items, did I summarise sections of the discussion?

Did I summarise the decisions reached?

Did I clearly identify the necessary actions following on from the decisions and those responsible for the actions?

Did I conclude the meeting on a positive note?

Did I meet with the minute-taker at the end of the meeting?

Summary

This chapter has focused on the role of the chairperson, considering the necessary activities which need to be undertaken before, during and after the meeting. As stated at the beginning of the chapter, the effectiveness of the chairperson has an impact, not just on the meeting itself, but on the minute-taking process as well. A strong relationship between minute-taker and chairperson can work wonders! The minute-taker feels more relaxed, confident and in control of the process, whereas the chairperson feels confident that an accurate set of draft minutes will be produced. That said, such a relationship needs to be developed and nurtured. This is not always easy and takes time and patience. It certainly requires a proactive stance on the part of the minute-taker, but any effort expended will be more than compensated by the 'smoother' minute-taking process which results.

Of course, developing a good relationship with the chairperson is only part of the process. Indeed, a minute-taker may be required to minute many meetings in the course of a typical month. These meetings may vary considerably in terms of the subject matter being discussed and the participants involved. Also, each meeting might have a different chairperson! In such a situation, how can the minute-taker develop a strategy for effective note-taking? This will be discussed in the following chapter.

5
Developing a strategy for effective note-taking

We can all conjure up an image of the hapless 'have notepad will travel' minute-taker, stumbling from one meeting to the next, furiously scribbling down notes at every turn. Although some sympathy can be extended to those who find themselves in this position, sticking to this approach is not to be encouraged! The note-taking phase is really the 'core' of the minute-taking process, because it provides the foundation for the production of the final minutes. However, it is 'locked' within a broader minute-taking framework which includes important tasks to be carried out before, during and after the meeting. If these tasks are not carried out effectively, the quality of the notes may suffer and, by extension, the quality and accuracy of the final minutes. For example, if a meeting will include discussion on a complex topic, a failure to undertake adequate research *prior* to the meeting may affect the quality of the notes taken. Similarly, if some discussion points require further clarification *following* the meeting, a failure to seek clarification may lead to an inaccurate set of draft minutes. Therefore, to be effective, minute takers need to think ahead and prepare well.

Throughout this book, the importance of preparation is emphasised (e.g. there are numerous references to activities which need to be carried out *before* the meeting, the value of *personal* preparation is featured in Chapter 7 and the checklists in Appendix 2 provide further reminders). However, this chapter examines the value of adopting a holistic approach at the outset through the creation of a *strategic framework* not only for note-taking, but also for the entire minute-taking process. This involves having a full understanding of the nature and requirements of *each* meeting. This will necessitate an understanding of the meeting 'cycle' and the identification of the challenges unique to each of the meetings you minute. Armed with this information, you will be able to craft a 'tailored' strategy for each of your meetings, involving all the necessary activities which need to be carried out before, during and after the meeting in relation to note-taking and the production and dissemination of the final minutes.

The importance of a strategic approach

A strategic approach facilitates the achievement of objectives. For example, a football team will compete in many matches over the course of a season, but each match will require a different strategy. If the strategy is well-formulated and closely followed, there is a greater chance of achieving the desired result. A commercial organisation may serve many different markets with its products or services. Creating a strategic focus for each market will contribute towards achieving a competitive advantage. In the same way, when minute takers treat each meeting as unique and develop a strategy for each one, there is a greater likelihood of a smoother minute-taking process … and less stress!

Developing a strategy for each meeting

Developing a strategy for each meeting requires considerable thought. Some activities will be common to all meetings; others will be more specific to individual meetings. In addition to administrative issues, you will need to consider 'people' factors such as the effectiveness of the chairperson and the roles and personalities of the participants. You will also need to determine the level of detail required in terms of note-taking and any requirement for reading and/or discussion with the participants prior to the meeting.

> **STOP AND THINK**
>
> Before reading on, take a few minutes to complete the following exercise.
>
> Think about a meeting where you take the minutes on a regular basis. Then on a piece of paper make three lists as follows:
>
> (a) list of all the activities required for the meeting from your perspective as a minute-taker (include activities before, during and after);
> (b) list of the problems and challenges which always seem to arise at this particular meeting; and
> (c) list of possible solutions to the problems and challenges identified in (b) above.

How did you get on? Depending on the length of your lists, you may feel more stressed now than when you started! Hopefully though, you'll appreciate the value of the exercise; it's a really good way to begin thinking about all the necessary minute-taking tasks relating to a meeting, from which you can then develop a structured approach.

You have probably concluded that some of the activities identified were generic and would apply to *any* meeting, whereas others related specifically to the meeting under review. You may have also discovered that some of the challenges and issues identified would be impossible to resolve in the short-term (e.g. problems caused by corporate culture or the personalities of individuals). The reality is that many of the challenges faced by the minute-taker relate to *people* and the way they behave. These factors also need to be taken into account when developing your strategic approach.

The following section provides a step-by-step guide to developing a targeted approach for each of the meetings you minute. It is recognised that, as a minute-taker, you will probably service a number of different meetings within a calendar year. Many of these will fall into a cyclical pattern (e.g. weekly, monthly, quarterly or annually). In addition, you may be required to minute various ad hoc meetings which fit around the established cycle. Ensure that *all* identifiable meetings are included in your planning framework.

Developing your strategy: A step-by-step guide

Step 1: Create a computer-held filing system

A well-developed strategy is not much use unless you can periodically remind yourself what it is! So, the first step is to create a folder headed 'minute-taking strategy' and then a series of clearly labelled sub-folders; one for each meeting. These folders will constitute a repository for all the reference material you develop. Your goal – with regard to each meeting – is to produce the following:

- a comprehensive checklist of all the activities which you, as a minute-taker, need to undertake; and
- additional supporting material which will help you to effectively carry out the activities on the checklist.

Step 2: Establish the meeting cycle for each meeting

The starting point for developing your comprehensive list of activities is to determine the meeting cycle for each of your meetings. The best way to approach this is to develop a generic cycle which can then be adapted for each meeting. A typical meeting cycle (from the perspective of the minute-taker) may look like this:

EXAMPLE

The meeting cycle: A generic framework

Undertake all necessary administrative tasks for the meeting (room booking, attendees, equipment etc.)
↓
Establish the deadline for submission of agenda items and supporting papers
↓
Prepare the agenda in draft form
↓
Arrange for approval of the agenda by the chairperson
↓
Collate all supporting paperwork
↓
Dispatch the agenda and supporting papers
↓
Meet with the chairperson prior to the meeting
↓
Undertake personal preparation for the meeting
↓
Attend the meeting and take the notes
↓

> **EXAMPLE continued**
>
> Meet with the chairperson following the meeting
> ↓
> Prepare the draft minutes
> ↓
> Proof-read the draft minutes
> ↓
> Send the draft minutes to the chairperson for approval
> ↓
> Receive back the draft minutes with amendments
> ↓
> Make corrections to the draft minutes
> ↓
> Circulate the final version of the minutes
>
> Following dispatch of the minutes, the administrative tasks for the next meeting can begin, thus completing the cycle.

The procedure for Step 2 then is as follows: First, develop your own generic framework. Second, copy the framework into each of your meeting files as a form of template. Finally, adapt the template for each meeting; this may involve adding, deleting or amending some of the activities and inserting dates etc.

So, at the end of Step 2 you have a high-level activity framework for each of your meetings with activities listed in chronological order. At this point, the activity checklist for each of your meetings will probably look quite *similar*, notwithstanding any adaptations made. However, meetings can vary considerably in terms of the demands made on the minute-taker and these demands need to be reflected in your checklists if they are to be of practical value. This issue is addressed in Step 3.

Step 3: Create a minute-taking strategy map

Each meeting you minute will pose challenges, but some meetings will pose far more challenges than others! A strategy map is a useful tool for illustrating the 'difficulty-level' for each of your meetings.

There are many factors which make a meeting difficult to minute, but the two predominant ones are:

- effectiveness (or otherwise) of the chairperson; and
- the level of detail required in the notes.

The reason why these two factors are particularly important is that so many of the other issues relate to them. For example, minute-takers experience problems:

- when little pre-meeting guidance is given on complex topic areas;
- where the objectives for each agenda item lack clarity;
- when the contributions of participants are difficult to understand;
- where decisions and actions are unclear;
- where summaries of key points are lacking;
- where timings are not adhered to; and
- when draft minutes are returned late.

The impact of all of these issues can be minimised when the chairperson is effective. Also, the level of detail required in the notes will determine the necessary amount of pre-meeting reading and research and post-meeting discussions with the chair and other participants. In addition, It will determine the level of concentration required at the meeting itself and the allocation of time for production of the final minutes including any necessary adjustments and corrections.

So, begin the process by plotting each of your meetings on a strategy map in relation to these two factors. A completed strategy map is shown in Figure 5.1 below:

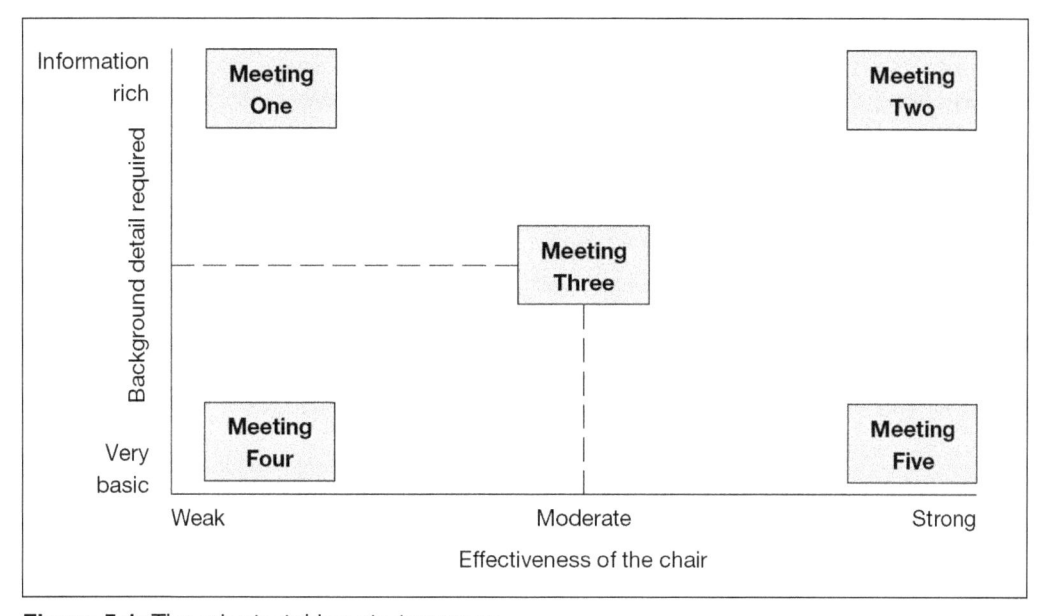

Figure 5.1: The minute-taking strategy map

This is a fairly straightforward model to construct (it can be a simple freehand drawing) and is a useful tool for creating an initial 'snapshot' of potential levels of difficulty. You can make the model as detailed as you wish in terms of the rating scales. In this example, the 'background detail required' ranges from 'very basic' to 'information-rich' and the 'effectiveness of the chair' from 'weak' to 'strong'. If you have been minuting your meetings for some time, then your assessment of the level of detail required should be reasonably straightforward. The same is true regarding the effectiveness of the chair, although your evaluation will necessarily be a little more subjective. That said, it is important to make your assessment as objective as possible: like or dislike for the chairperson should not be the sole criterion! It might be a good idea to make a list of the criteria which you feel are important (see Chapter 4) and use this as the basis for your evaluation. If you are minuting a meeting for the first time, then you can make some initial evaluations and revise them subsequently if necessary.

Next, *analyse the results*. The overall objective is to arrive at a list of actions which can be incorporated into the activity list produced as the outcome of Step 2. In the example given above, 'Meeting Five' appears relatively straightforward, the level of detail is basic and the chairperson is strong. Therefore, there may be few additional actions to add. However, even though the level of detail is basic, if this was a meeting where, for example, participants were likely to employ the use of jargon and technical terms, it might be advisable to prepare a reference note as an aid to understanding and keep it in the file (this will be discussed in Step 7). So, in this example, a possible action to add to the list could be to 'review the technical terms reference note, prior to the meeting'.

A glance at 'Meeting One' suggests the meeting from hell! Detailed notes are required and the chairperson is very weak. Additional actions would be required here. Due to the necessity for a high level of background detail, possible actions could be to:

- review the technical terms reference note, prior to the meeting;
- meet with participants prior to the meeting to check understanding;
- meet with participants following the meeting to seek clarifications;
- fully review the previous set of minutes prior to the meeting;
- fully read all supporting papers prior to the meeting;
- read additional material which may aid understanding of the topic; and
- review the objectives for each agenda item.

Because of the problems with the weak chairperson, possible actions could be to:

- remind the chairperson of all meeting cycle timescales;
- ensure that the agenda has clear objectives and appropriate timings;
- remind the chairperson to summarise at the end of each agenda item;
- alert the chairperson if pre-set timings begin to slip; and
- interrupt during the meeting to seek clarification if necessary.

Meeting One and Meeting Five are the two 'extremes'. Of course, the other three meetings in the example would all require some additional actions, to a greater or lesser degree. When you undertake this exercise for your own meetings, you will naturally arrive at a list of action points for each one derived from the analysis of your minute-taking strategy map. At this point you will have two lists for *each* of your meetings: (a) the list of activities in chronological order (the outcome from Step 2), and (b) the list of additional actions (derived from the minute-taking strategy map) (the outcome from Step 3).

Step 4: Amalgamate the output from steps 2 and 3 and compile a list in chronological order

This step simply involves an amalgamation of the two lists. Aim to maintain the chronological order. Obviously, some judgement is required (e.g. an action such as: '*Interrupt during the meeting to seek clarification if necessary'* could happen at any point during the meeting, but it will still happen *during* the meeting). An action such as: *'Remind the chairperson of all meeting cycle timescales'* could appear more than once and be specific (e.g. as an action *before* the meeting in connection with the approval of the agenda and as an action *after* the meeting in connection with receipt of the amended minutes).

After completing Step 4, you will have a fairly well-developed list of activities for each of your meetings reflecting both standard activities and those which are unique to each meeting.

Step 5: Brainstorm any additional activities and any sub-sets of activities to add to your list produced in step 4

In Step 5, you have the opportunity to develop your list even further. Think hard about any activities which may have been overlooked (e.g. are you required at any of your meetings to act both as minute-taker and contributor?) If so, there may be additional activities to add (see Chapter 2). For the sake of completeness, it is also worth scanning the generic reminder checklists in Appendix 2. Also, you may feel that some of the larger activities on the list need to be broken down into a series of smaller tasks.

Step 6: Compile a final, 'master' list of activities in chronological order

Now compile your 'master' checklist for each meeting by integrating the additional activities identified during Step 5.

Step 7: Create a series of additional reference documents specific to the meeting

Your final document will be a valuable reference tool because it constitutes a comprehensive checklist, in chronological order, of all the activities you need to undertake for each of the meetings you minute. However, it is still just a list of activities: *you* have to carry them out! Step 7 involves adding some additional documents to your file for each meeting which will help you to carry out your note-taking and minute-writing tasks.

Although not an exhaustive list, points (a) to (i) below provide some examples of information which will be of use to you:

(a) relevant reference material;
(b) a list of words in 'personalised shorthand' to assist in note-taking;
(c) a list of useful abbreviations and symbols to assist in note-taking;
(d) a list of technical terms and jargon;
(e) the written output (observations and actions) from the strategy map exercise;
(f) information about meeting participants;
(g) past minutes;
(h) a list of useful words and phrases to assist in minute-writing; and
(i) a minutes template (if applicable).

Points (a) and (d) are important because a review prior to the meeting of reference material relating to the topics which will be discussed and any technical terms which are likely to be used in the discussions, will aid understanding during the note-taking phase (particularly useful where the requirement for background detail is high). Likewise, the use of personalised shorthand and abbreviations will make the note-taking task easier in such meetings (points (b) and (c) will be examined in greater detail in Chapter 8).

Your notes from the strategy map exercise are also worth collating and filing. Apart from the actions – which will have been integrated into your checklist – you will have notes on, for example, the strengths and weaknesses of the chairperson. These are worth keeping and referring to periodically as you seek to develop your relationship with the chairperson over time. That said you may need to exercise a degree of caution. Under the Data Protection Act your notes may need to be shared!

Point (f) is an interesting one. It was mentioned previously that many of the problems encountered in the minute-taking process relate to people and their behaviour. Many of the activities on your master checklist will involve interaction with people: often the chairperson, but also the participants. For example, you may need to approach certain individuals to seek clarifications either before or after the meeting. During the meeting itself you may need to interrupt to seek clarification on a point. As noted in Chapter 4, a range of 'colourful' personalities are on display at most meetings and participants are unlikely to modify their approach just to make it easier for you to take the notes! Views will be expressed loudly, quietly, aggressively, sarcastically, enthusiastically, reluctantly and incoherently – and you have to make sense of it all!

The suggestion here is to give some thought to the personality types evident in each of your meetings and consider how these will impact on effective communication. Consider these questions: Is your job as minute-taker made harder in some cases because of personality-related issues? Are some expressions made in the meeting particularly hard to understand? Are important points often obscured due to poor communication skills? Do you find that you miss the essence of an argument despite the chairperson's best efforts to summarise? Are some of the participants difficult to communicate with one-to-one? Are some participants unapproachable?

Make notes on the above for each of your meetings and keep them in your strategy file (if your thoughts are put down *in writing* you have a good reminder tool to review when preparing for the meeting). Although there are no magical solutions to personality-related communication problems; simply identifying and *reflecting* on the issues can help you focus on how to address them. For example, if you know that certain participants tend to 'pad-out' their comments with irrelevancies, but get to the point eventually, then you can remind yourself to focus your concentration and not 'switch-off'. If you know some participants are highly emotional and/or aggressive when making their contributions, but make valid points, then you can remind yourself to focus on *what* is said, not *the way* it is said. If some participants are difficult to communicate with one-to-one, you can remind yourself to think more deeply about the reasons why and perhaps adapt your own communication style. You may also benefit from sharing your thoughts with the chairperson and exploring practical solutions in your pre-meeting.

To kick-start your thinking, undertake the 'Stop and Think' exercise below. You can then use this as a framework to develop your notes for all your other meetings. An important point to note: Your overall findings may be quite revealing. Your notes will reflect *your* opinions, views and judgements on a range of 'people issues'. Remember that these notes are designed to help you do your job better. they are for your eyes only, so ensure they are kept on a password-protected computer!

> STOP AND THINK
>
> Think of a meeting where you take the minutes on a regular basis and consider the following questions:
>
> What personality types are evident in the participant group?
>
> Do any personality types pose challenges for you as you undertake your minute-taking duties? If so, what are the challenges?
>
> What strategies could you devise to minimise the impact of the personality-related communication problems you have experienced?

Points (g), (h) and (i) in the list above relate to documents that will be helpful in *minute writing*. A review of the previous minutes will provide reminders on layout and style (this can also be helpful in pre-meeting preparation), a list of useful words and phrases will assist in composition and the use of the template (pre-populated to the extent possible) will save valuable time.

The notes for points (b), (c) and (h) will necessarily take time and effort to develop; however, some detailed guidelines and examples are provided for you in Chapters 8 and 9.

Step 8: Review the strategy file for each meeting prior to preparation

At the conclusion of steps 1–7, you will have a *completed strategy file* (computer-held) for each of the meetings you minute. For each meeting you will have a comprehensive checklist of activities, tailored to the precise requirements of that meeting. You will also have a set of supporting reference documents that will assist you in carrying out the activities effectively.

The strategy file will have taken time and effort to compile, so make your investment worthwhile; consult it regularly!

Step 9: Monitor, review and amend

Regularly review your checklist and notes for each meeting. Things will inevitably change over time; members may leave, new members may join, some groups may be disbanded, new meeting structures may emerge. Ensure that any necessary amendments are made so that your notes remain current and of value.

Step 10: Maintain a focus on personal skills development

As you develop your lists and supporting notes – and indeed by reflecting on your own experience to date – you'll no doubt recognise that performing the minute-taking role effectively, requires a broad skill base. As you perform your minute-taking tasks, take time to reflect on your performance and try to isolate any skills *gaps*. Then take appropriate steps to address them.

You may find that some of these gaps relate to interpersonal issues such as self-confidence and assertiveness. Chapters 12, 13 and 14 explore these areas in more detail and emphasise the importance of ongoing skills development.

Summary

The chapter has emphasised the importance of developing a targeted strategy for each of the meetings you are required to minute and has outlined a ten-step process for achieving this. Completing the process for all your meetings will necessitate some hard work up front, but if you are prepared to make the effort you will be rewarded with a far clearer picture of what you are aiming to achieve and some well-thought-through strategies to support you. In turn, this should increase your confidence in your ability to perform all duties effectively. Remember that the process outlined is just a guide; feel free to adapt it – in terms of detail and content – to suit your personal and organisational requirements.

One key activity of course – whatever the nature of the meeting – is the preparation of the *agenda*. Just how much thought should go into this? What are the benefits of a well-constructed agenda and what are the potential implications of working with a poor one? How can an effective agenda contribute towards a successful meeting? How can a good agenda assist both the chairperson and the minute-taker? How can it benefit the participants? What are the key principles underpinning the creation of an effective agenda? What are the key pitfalls to avoid? Should the agenda follow a set style? Who is responsible for creating the agenda? Is the any other business item (AOB) absolutely necessary? All these questions will be answered in Chapter 6.

6
The agenda

Imagine that you have bought an expensive new coat and have worn it for the first time. When you arrive home and take it off, would you throw it on the floor and leave it there until you need it again? Of course not! You would carefully place it on a coat hanger and hang it in a wardrobe to keep it clean. Why use the coat hanger? Because it helps to avoid creases and thus preserves the shape of your coat. You could say that your coat maintains its shape because it is hanging on two *key points* (i.e. both ends of the coat hanger).

Now, think of a meeting that you are required to minute. For the meeting to be effective, it needs to maintain its 'shape' (i.e. it needs a clear structure). That structure is provided by the agenda. It could be said that the meeting maintains its shape because it 'hangs' on a number of key points (i.e. the agenda items).

Apart from providing structure, the agenda has other purposes.

Benefits of a good agenda

The benefits of a good agenda can be summarised as follows:

- It provides a clear structure for the meeting as illustrated above
- It provides a foundation for advance preparation:
  - For the chairperson
  - For the participants
  - For the minute-taker

- It allows the chairperson to plan in advance how to manage:
  - Challenging items
  - Potential problem areas
  - Objectives of each item
  - Time allocation
  - Time management

- It provides a clear structure for the minute-taker (taking notes and writing minutes).

Unfortunately, many agendas fail to reach these ideal standards, so they are not as effective as they could be.

> **STOP AND THINK**
>
> Think about the meetings in your organisation; particularly the meetings you minute:
>
> Is the agenda for each one constructed effectively? What things work well? Are there any areas which you feel could be improved and why?

You were probably able to identify at least a few areas for improvement, but many meeting organisers continue with the same approach towards agenda preparation, sometimes for years! This is fine if best practice principles are followed, but if not, the meeting could be failing to maximise the benefits of a tool which – if prepared well – can prove to be a real asset.

Constructing a good agenda

So, what factors are essential in the constructing of an effective agenda?

Giving notice and inviting contributions

Rules and practice vary, both across and within organisations, regarding the notice period for a meeting and the involvement participants may have in contributing agenda items for discussion. For example, the Companies Act 2006 makes no provision regarding notice of directors' meetings. However, under the common law, reasonable notice must be given to all directors. The company's articles of association usually specify the method for serving the notice (e.g. in written form, by telephone etc.) and the agenda may be included as part of the notice.

There are various types of meeting where the topics for discussion may be already decided. For example, a management meeting may be called via e-mail specifically to deal with an emergency matter. In such cases, the agenda is already fixed and the date for the meeting may be predetermined. For some one-off meetings, participants may be invited to submit agenda items; this invitation would usually form part of the notice. For regular meetings, the final item on the agenda of the previous meeting will have been: *Date of the next meeting*. This is a good opportunity to remind the group of the deadline date for submission of agenda items.

When discussing the meeting cycle in Chapter 5, the need to establish the deadline for submission of agenda items and accompanying papers was emphasised. *If it is the practice* for the meetings you minute to invite contributions to the agenda, the key point to remember is this: The agenda will be more effective when members of the group are given *sufficient time* to think about possible items for inclusion.

Responsibility for preparation

For many types of meeting, the chairperson and the minute-taker work closely together in the preparation of the agenda. As a proactive minute-taker, it will benefit you greatly if you become involved in preparing the draft agenda, perhaps by taking on the task of arranging the items into a logical order ready for final approval by the chairperson. By doing this, you will acquire a 'feel' for the meeting, which will enable you to develop your strategy for personal preparation in a more targeted way.

Creating the agenda

What should the agenda look like? Well, the order of the agenda will be pre-determined to a certain degree, because most meetings will follow a recognised structure (see Chapter 3). An example agenda is shown below.

EXAMPLE

CONFERENCE PLANNING COMMITTEE MEETING

Tuesday 20 November 2018
10:00–13:00
Training Room, Regency House

AGENDA

1. Apologies for absence
2. Minutes of the previous meeting
3. Matters arising
4. Information only
5. Conference agenda
6. Keynote speaker
7. Facilities and services
8. Conference pack
9. Any other business
10. Date of next meeting

Does this look like a good agenda to you? At first glance it seems fine. It's neatly laid out and the name of the group, date, time and place of the meeting are all provided in the heading. The agenda items are clearly listed and appear to follow a logical order. Many meetings use an agenda in a style similar to this. However, if you take a closer look there are some points to note. Apart from the heading, there is no detail about each of the items, so the specific points for discussion under each heading are not clear. Some members may have contributed points for discussion in relation to these themes, so *they* know both what the topic is and that they are leading on that part if the item – but nobody else does! This means that members cannot get a sense of how the overall meeting is likely to unfold and what the main objectives are, thus limiting the degree of meaningful preparation. For example, under the item *'conference agenda'*, what exactly will be discussed? Members can only guess: it could be a simple discussion about who will coordinate it, or it may involve a deeper discussion regarding the topics for inclusion and the key presenters.

Also, the overall time allocated for the meeting is three hours. How will this be divided up between the various items? There is no indication on the agenda at all. So, what can be done to make this agenda more effective?

Sub-dividing agenda items and creating a logical order

If the meeting is chaired effectively, the early sections of the meeting should be concluded relatively quickly. This allows the majority of the available time to be utilised in discussion of the main agenda items. However, the grouping of the main agenda items will require careful thought. So, placing these items into a logical order for discussion is a key initial task. Following this, the main headings should be further sub-divided to show the specific sub-items that will be discussed under each of the main subject headings. These also should be listed based on a logical order for discussion. Ideally it is best to deal with the most important items first when minds are still relatively alert. Also, there may be a natural link between items, so think about the logical flow very carefully. When the logical order has been determined, the names of the lead contributors should be added against each of the sub-items.

Inclusion of objectives

This is an important point. If the minutes tell the members *where they've been*, then logically, the agenda needs to tell them *where they're going*! The whole purpose of a meeting is to take decisions and decide on who will carry out any agreed actions. Therefore, it makes sense that the members are focused on what these decisions will involve at the earliest possible stage. This is not difficult to do. For example, if one of the agreed sub-items under the conference agenda heading is '*Key presenters*', then simply re-word it to include the specific objective (e.g. '*to select key presenters*'). Explicitly stating the objectives has a number of advantages as follows:

- participants know what the purpose of each sub-item is so they can prepare in a more focused way;
- at the meeting itself, contributions are likely to be sharper and more to the point;
- the chairperson knows what the exact purpose of each sub-item is, so can concentrate on managing the discussion to ensure that all necessary objectives are achieved;
- the chairperson will have a clearer understanding of possible contentious issues relating to the achievement of the objectives (e.g. any 'hidden agendas') so will be better placed to deal with them, either prior to the meeting or on the day;
- the minute-taker knows what the key objectives are at the outset, so it will be easier to identify the decisions. This should make it easier to listen to the discussion and to recognise the elements which are necessary to note in relation to the key decisions. In turn this will help to reduce stress levels because there is no need to take copious notes in the fear that something may be missed;

- should any important points be overlooked by the chairperson during the meeting, it is easier for the minute-taker to provide any needed prompts;
- the minute-taker can walk out of the meeting room confident that all the key decisions and actions have been recorded. This will make writing up of the final minutes a more straightforward exercise than it might otherwise have been.

Inclusion of timings

Time management is very important in a meeting. There are three points to note in this regard:

1. The overall time allocated for the meeting should be observed; the meeting should start and finish on time.
2. Sufficient time should be allocated for the discussion on each main agenda item.
3. Sufficient time should be allocated for the discussion on each agenda sub-item.

It would seem, therefore, to make good sense to *include the timings* for each item on the agenda. In theory at least, such an approach encourages succinct contributions from participants and reminds the chairperson to move the discussion on, where necessary, in the interests of good time management. The practice of placing timings on an agenda works well in conjunction with the inclusion of the objectives; people know where they're going and also when they're expected to arrive there! However, this approach does require a professional attitude from all concerned; if this doesn't materialise, then the inclusion of timings will be pointless.

As a proactive minute-taker, if you perceive that the lack of good time management is affecting the quality of your meetings, take the initiative in trying to promote change. Will this work? Well, have a read of the following case study:

CASE STUDY

Anne-Marie undertook a range of secretarial duties for a medium-sized consultancy company where she had worked for 15 years. She was a very experienced minute-taker, and regularly took the minutes at board and management meetings.

During her time at the company, she had earned a good reputation as a solid professional who could be relied upon to always carry out her duties to a very high standard. She was also very proactive: despite all her experience, she decided to book herself on a one-day minute-taking course as a refresher!

During the course she participated thoroughly, freely sharing all her knowledge and experience with the rest of the group. The final session of the morning addressed the preparation of the agenda. The trainer discussed the issue of using a timed agenda and strongly advocated that the delegates be proactive and push to initiate change. At that point Anne-Marie took hold of the course agenda and threw it in the air! 'A timed agenda, a timed agenda – you must be crazy; there's no way in a million years that my board would ever accept an agenda with timings on it!'

> ### CASE STUDY continued
>
> The somewhat bemused trainer then ventured to ask why. Anne-Marie responded: 'As far as they're concerned, it takes as long as it takes and that's it. It's always been that way – yes, it's really frustrating but it'll never change; no way!' The trainer then asked if Anne-Marie was the only person in that particular meeting who felt strongly about the issue. 'Well, the chairman gets a bit fed up at times' she replied. At that point, the 'call for lunch' came and the discussion ended.
>
> About three months after the course, the trainer received an unexpected e-mail from Anne-Marie. In part, it said: 'Guess what? When I got back to the office I started to think about what you said and I went up to the chairman and told him we needed to do something about the timing problem; he agreed! I decided that it might be a step too far to include the timings on the main agenda initially so I prepared a separate chair's agenda with the timings on it that only he (and I) could see. I didn't put the length of the items, just the concluding time for each one. We've had three meetings since then and they're so much better – the chairman is really working to control the contributions and keep everything on track. We haven't got a wall clock in the room, so I even bought him a mini-clock which he places on the table so only he and I can see it! Things are changing – and the members are none the wiser!'

Case analysis

The case clearly illustrates the benefit of addressing the time management issue. In this scenario, real improvement in the management of the meeting was achieved. Whether Anne-Marie should now push for timings to appear on the main agenda is a debatable point. Some might say that if the situation is now working well; it is best left as it is to avoid 'rocking the boat'. Others might argue that things have improved only because the *chairperson* is managing the meeting more effectively. The meeting could improve even further if all members acknowledged the time constraints, because it would enable more focused preparation.

The case illustrates another important point: the value of being a proactive minute-taker! The decision to attend the course, the decision to approach the chairperson and the decision to buy the clock are all examples of taking the initiative: being proactive really can make a difference!

Any other business

Any other business (AOB) appears on just about every agenda produced, but is probably one of the most mishandled items on the entire agenda.

THE AGENDA

> **STOP AND THINK**
>
> 1. Does AOB appear on the agenda of all the meetings you minute?
> 2. If there are any meetings where it is not included, why is this?
> 3. In your experience, when it is included, is it usually handled well or poorly?
> 4. What principles do you think should govern the inclusion of AOB?
> 5. In your opinion, what factors characterise a poorly handled AOB item?

Just from a brief consideration of the above questions, you were probably able to identify quite a few negative factors. Even if some of your meetings are effective in the use of AOB, it is unlikely that *all* are. Unfortunately the term 'any other business' is just *too* accurate when applied to many meetings: the discussion really is about any *other* business (i.e. any business other than what should be being discussed at the meeting!). What are some of the problems that frequently occur?

- AOB becomes a 'talking shop' where anything and everything are discussed. including, in many cases, issues which are not strictly related to the purpose of the meeting;
- some members view this as the opportunity to 'have their say' on contentious issues;
- the chairperson may lose an element of control, particularly if exchanges become heated;
- if AOB items are just 'thrown in to the mix', members have had no time to prepare and the quality of the debate will suffer as a consequence;
- people will be tired by this point and will find it harder to concentrate. This can affect the quality of the discussion; a problem exacerbated the longer AOB continues;
- if AOB is continually mishandled and over-long, members may become frustrated and this can lead to irregular attendance;
- decisions may be made on important matters in haste;
- where discussions are characterised by heated debate and even arguments, relationships between group members can deteriorate over time;
- being aware of time constraints and that some members are seeking to leave, some members may take the opportunity to secure quickly-made decisions that suit their own hidden agendas; and
- the opportunity to freely submit items under AOB encourages a lackadaisical approach. If members can discuss whatever they like under AOB, then why worry about submitting agenda items on time?

So, what can be done to manage AOB effectively? The chairperson needs to be assertive in promoting best practice and *you*, as the proactive minute-taker, can help with this. What, though, *is* best practice? Well, think about the following question in connection with the decision to include an item under AOB:

Had this item been known about before the agenda was prepared and circulated, would it have been included in the agenda?

If the answer is yes, then it must be important and/or urgent. If the answer is no, then it isn't. The chairperson needs to make the decision as to what to include. What are the options? In Chapter 3, the 'DRAFT' mnemonic was shown in the *structure of a meeting* example, under the 'any other business' section. It is reproduced below.

> **EXAMPLE**
> - **D**efer to the next meeting
> - **R**eject it
> - **A**ccept as genuine AOB
> - **F**it into the agenda
> - **T**rash it?

The chairperson can choose to deal with possible AOB items in a number of ways. The item can be deferred to the next meeting, it can be rejected as being outside the purposes of the meeting, it can be accepted as genuine any other business or, in some cases, it may be possible to integrate it into an existing agenda item. However, all requests must be made known to the chairperson *prior to* the commencement of the meeting; this rule should be made absolutely clear to all and strictly adhered to by the chairperson.

In reality, very few important and/or urgent matters that would have formed the basis for an item on the agenda and would have been included had they been known about when the agenda was being prepared, suddenly arise just prior to the meeting! So, if this approach is applied rigorously, AOB should present no real problems. As a proactive minute-taker you can do much to encourage members to contribute their items on time (i.e. prior to the preparation of the draft agenda).

The last point in the mnemonic above is: 'Trash it?' This does not refer to rejecting the item on the day, it refers to the possibility of scrapping AOB altogether! Is this a realistic option? Please read the following case study.

> **CASE STUDY**
> Vanina was the secretary to the management board of a London-based hotel company. She was an experienced minute-taker and reasonably confident in the role. She was asked to attend a one-day minute-taking course in line with her continuous professional development.
>
> During discussions about the value of a well-thought-out agenda, the trainer asked if anyone had experienced major problems with the handling of AOB. Vanina chipped straight in with a resounding YES! She said: 'The problem with our board is that it's a meeting of "two halves". Everything tends to go really well for the main part of the meeting. We use a timed agenda and

CASE STUDY continued

the chair is effective at managing the contributions. Then AOB arrives and everything goes "pear-shaped". Everyone's got something to say and no one's prepared!'

The trainer then discussed with the group the true purpose of AOB (i.e. to discuss matters of a substantive nature that would have been on the agenda had they been known about at the time the agenda was prepared and dispatched). Vanina agreed that 'real' AOB didn't happen very often. Occasionally, an important and/or urgent matter did come to light following the dispatch of the agenda, but the chair usually knew about it and ensured that it was noted for AOB. Also, where possible, he would let members know in advance of the meeting to allow at least some time for preparation. She said that the real problem was the perennial 'free-for-all' which masquerades as genuine AOB! The trainer asked the question to the group: 'Have you ever thought of taking it off; scrapping AOB?' Vanina loved the idea, but said: 'Sounds great but if I ever suggested such a thing, blood would be spilled – mine!'

Interestingly, about six months later, Vanina sent an e-mail to the trainer, part of which read as follows: 'I did it, I actually did it! I said to the chair that I'd been on this course and they said that AOB should be scrapped and that we ought to do it. To my surprise he agreed that it was worth considering. We did it gradually to avoid an outcry – just kept reducing the items accepted and kept reminding people to get their items in on time. Then after a few meetings we left it off completely. People at last began to realise that they needed to get their items on at the draft stage, or they weren't going to get them on at all! Over the past month, several of the members have commented on how much they're really enjoying the meetings now!'

Case analysis

Vanina is a good example of a proactive minute-taker. She felt apprehensive about raising the issue, but she displayed courage and voiced her concerns. Then she worked closely with the chairperson to implement the new strategy. The case illustrates very well how an otherwise effective meeting can be 'hijacked' by the abuse of AOB. It may not always be practical to remove the item entirely (e.g. because it's not necessary to give notice of the business to be dealt with at board meetings, some matters which were not included in the agenda may need to be dealt with under AOB). However, there are still issues to consider here (e.g. preparation time is still needed). Some matters may need to be put to the vote under AOB. This could cause problems if the matter is controversial and some directors are not present. In such cases, it might be better to defer the decision making until the next meeting if it is non-urgent, or to hold an extra unscheduled board meeting if it is.

So, taking into account the points discussed in the various sections above, what might a well-prepared agenda look like?

EXAMPLE

CONFERENCE PLANNING COMMITTEE MEETING

Tuesday 20 November 2018
10:00–13:00
Training Room, Regency House

AGENDA

1. Apologies for absence
2. Minutes of the previous meeting — 10 mins
3. Matters arising — 10 mins
   - 3.1 Hotel booking — Ayesha Richards
   - 3.2 Catering arrangements — John Wescombe
   - 3.3 Transportation for overseas delegates — Ayesha Richards
4. Information only — 20 mins
   - 4.1 Financial report — Deepak Lawrence
   - 4.2 Media coverage — Sophie Denholm
   - 4.3 Health and safety — Tim Gardner
5. Conference agenda — 40 mins
   - 5.1 To discuss possible items — Dan Miller
   - 5.2 To discuss and agree strategic theme — Alex Williams
   - 5.3 To select key presenters
   - 5.4 To appoint agenda coordinator
6. Keynote speaker — 30 mins
   - 6.1 To select from shortlist
   - 6.2 To discuss and agree the key points of the speech
   - 6.3 To confirm timing for the keynote address
7. Facilities and services — 45 mins
   - 7.1 To discuss and agree IT requirements — Shahid Verma
   - 7.2 To agree the range of services for delegates — John Wescombe
       List of venue amenities attached
8. Conference Pack — 15 mins
   - 8.1 To discuss and agree design of conference bag — Sophie Denholm
   - 8.2 To discuss documentation required
       Draft attached
9. Any Other Business — 10 mins
10. Date of next meeting — 18 December 2018

The example encapsulates some of the main points discussed in this section. You will note that the main agenda items are broken down into specific objectives, the person leading the discussion on each of the items is named and the timings for each item are indicated. The timings indicated in this example relate to the actual *duration* of the items. Alternatively, you may choose to indicate the start and/or end times of each item. There are no rules; the key point is that the recording method you select must be the one that the chairperson feels most comfortable with in terms of keeping track of time.

Circulating the agenda

You need to maintain an up-to-date circulation list containing the names of everyone who is entitled to receive a copy of the agenda. The list will usually be comprised of the regular members and any one-off attendees. You may also choose to send a copy to any invited observers.

The agenda and accompanying papers obviously need to be dispatched in advance of the meeting, but just how far in advance will depend on the nature of the meeting. Using the example of an AGM, it should be noted that, for companies, there are statutory minimum notice periods. On the other hand, a one-off meeting, arranged due to an emergency issue, would have a far shorter lead time. Ideally, for most regular meetings, it is good to aim for at least a week. This will give participants the chance to reflect on the agenda and read through the relevant paperwork.

All relevant paperwork should be attached to the agenda when dispatched. For some meetings you may want to mark the papers to indicate its agenda item number. Notes can also be made on the agenda referring to the relevant report. Accompanying papers can be problematic: sometimes the paperwork is voluminous so, for certain meetings, you might want to consider sending some of the information electronically. Also, the information often goes unread. This is not just because of the amount of papers to read through, but because of the poor quality of papers in terms of communication style. As a proactive minute-taker, try to encourage members –perhaps in conjunction with the chairperson – to think about how a paper would be perceived by a person reading it. Is it clear how it relates to the agenda item? Does it communicate the message effectively?

Summary

In this chapter, the preparation of the agenda has been examined in detail. Various points were made regarding how to construct a meaningful agenda that clearly tells participants *'where they are going'*. The benefits of building the agenda around the meeting's objectives and the value of including timings were both emphasised and you were also encouraged to critically analyse the value of AOB at your meetings and, if necessary, to assertively offer suggestions for change!

Preparation of the agenda is only one part, albeit an important part, of preparing for a meeting. Further aspects including the need for personal preparation are addressed in Chapter 7.

7
The importance of personal preparation

Have you ever been asked to deliver a business presentation at relatively short notice? If you have, you'll no doubt recall the sense of apprehension – if not total panic – that sets in. In a presentation, you are very exposed; all eyes are upon you and, if you are poorly prepared, you are unlikely to give of your best.

The old adage that 'if you fail to prepare, you are preparing to fail' holds true in most situations in life. There are some situations where you can 'get away' with surface-level preparation and still give a reasonable account of yourself – taking minutes at a meeting is not one of them!

In Chapter 5, you were encouraged to develop a tailored strategy for each of the meetings you minute consisting of a detailed checklist, in chronological order, of all the activities you need to undertake for the entire minute-taking process. This chapter focuses on some of the key activities which need to take place *prior* to the meeting. All of these activities should be included in the checklist you prepare for each meeting, so if you've read Chapter 5 and have already started to prepare your lists, this chapter will provide a few detailed reminders to assist you. A key preparatory activity is the preparation and circulation of the agenda and accompanying paperwork. This area was discussed in detail in the previous chapter, so is excluded here.

In terms of a timeline, the activities discussed in the chapter begin with the initial administration arrangements for the meeting and conclude with activities which take place just prior to the actual *commencement of the meeting*. Depending on the nature of your role, you may not be actively involved in all these activities, but taking a proactive stance, you'll be keen to ensure that all preparatory activities take place in a systematic and orderly way and to exert whatever influence you can to make this happen. Two main areas will be discussed as follows:

1. general administrative arrangements; and
2. personal preparation.

General administrative arrangements

Attendees and notice

The level of effort required to set up a meeting varies considerably. Some meetings may be planned a year in advance, with a clearly established set of dates and the meeting venue pre-booked for the duration. Other meetings will require far more 'running around' to agree dates, book rooms and determine who the attendees are. As a start point, then, it is essential to determine who should attend the meeting.

For regular meetings there should be a readily accessible membership list and a record of attendees from previous meetings. Keep this list in your strategy file for each meeting and ensure that it is regularly updated. It would also be advantageous to keep a record of all the contact details for each attendee and to amend and update the details when necessary. For some meetings, observers may be invited and it is important that they are informed of the time and place of the meeting and the reasons they have been asked to attend. They should also be reminded that they are there to observe and not to contribute. From time to time it is quite likely that people who are not members of the group will be invited to attend the meeting and participate. This may happen for a variety of reasons (e.g. at a departmental meeting, a senior manager may be invited to explain the details of a major policy change, or a representative of a health and safety committee may be invited to deliver a presentation on changes to current practice). Some attendees may be invited for the entire meeting, some for just one part only. It is important that all attendees invited on a one-off basis are fully informed of the administrative arrangements and why they have been invited to attend. They should also be asked if they have any special requirements in terms of facilities and equipment.

One-off meetings will probably present more of a challenge in terms of logistics. Rooms and equipment may not be readily available, it may be difficult to agree dates and there may be some uncertainty over who should be invited. Work closely with the chairperson in such situations and be proactive in contacting participants to secure dates, inform them of what is expected and find out about any special requirements.

Aim to provide as much notice as possible to allow for the submission of agenda items and supporting papers. This will allow for the dispatch of the final agenda and accompanying papers in good time. Some meetings will require additional preparation, reading and research on the part of participants, so adequate notice is required to ensure that all the deadlines inherent in the meeting cycle are adhered to. This will enable participants to come to the meeting well prepared and ready to contribute in a meaningful way.

Venue and equipment

It is in your best interest that the meeting is conducted effectively because that will make it easier for you to take notes without unnecessary distraction. Even when the chairperson is effective and the participants are engaged, it can still be difficult for all to concentrate if the facilities are inadequate. This aspect is sometimes underestimated and meetings are often held in rooms which are just not fit for purpose. Much depends, of course, on the size of the organisation's premises, the internal structure of the offices and rooms and the demands made for space. Some organisations operate a *space management unit*, a department responsible for allocating space and managing the competing demands for it. Finding a suitable room can be a particular problem when a meeting is called at short notice. In such situations, some compromises may have to be made or consideration given to using an external venue if the importance of the meeting justifies that.

Take a look at the *meeting room checklist* in the box below. These are some of the important points to consider when booking the room and then ensuring that it is laid out correctly. Gauging the noise level is particularly important. A meeting room situated just above a busy street will be a distraction. However, often the distraction is more off-putting if it is in the immediate environment. Meetings in open plan office spaces can be problematic and rooms just off busy corridors or near photocopiers and/or kitchen facilities are not ideal.

> ## CHECKLIST
>
> ### Meeting room: checklist
>
> - Is it suitable for the size of the group?
> - Is it well-ventilated?
> - Is it well-lit?
> - What is the noise level?
> - Is the layout correct for this type of meeting?
> - What refreshments will be required?
> - Are there enough power sockets?
> - Are name plates required?
> - Is all necessary equipment available?
> - Is all equipment in good working order?
> - Is a lectern or microphone required?
> - Is the seating comfortable?
> - What 'accessories' are required for the table?

The availability of equipment is also a key factor, particularly where people are invited to give presentations or where video-conferencing facilities are needed. It is not just the availability which is important but the reliability. There is nothing more frustrating for all concerned than equipment that breaks down intermittently or just doesn't work! Think also about the layout of the room. The traditional oval table set-up may be fine, but an alternative layout may be needed if the meeting involves an element of group-based brainstorming and problem-solving activities.

The necessary paperwork

On the day of the meeting, ensure that all the necessary paperwork is at hand. This includes not only your own requirements (which will be discussed in the personal preparation section) but also the potential requirements of the attendees. In this regard you should make sure that you have:

- spare copies of the agenda;
- spare copies of the accompanying paperwork;
- spare copies of the minutes from the previous meeting; and
- a copy of the constitution and/or any rules that apply to the meeting.

Depending on the practice in your organisation, you may also need to take a copy of the minutes for signing. At board meetings for example, the minutes are usually signed by the chairperson of the next succeeding board meeting.

The final check

All the issues on the meeting room checklist will have been dealt with sometime prior to the meeting. Now, on the day, it is important to carry out a final check to ensure all arrangements are in place. Make sure that the refreshments have definitely been ordered and will arrive on time. Also check that the equipment is in the room and is in good working order. Ensure that the layout of the room is correct and that all the necessary items are laid out on the table (e.g. water, glasses, paper and pens).

Attendance details

You will need accurate details from the meeting regarding attendance so take a few minutes prior to the start of the meeting to address this. Take with you the list of people you expect to attend. Also take a signing-in sheet for people to sign when they arrive. You should also have a list of all who have sent apologies. You will need to distinguish between those who are present (members), those who are in attendance (attending but not a member), any observers and any substitutions (attending on behalf of someone). Try to have this information organised as much as possible before the meeting starts; you can then liaise with the chairperson to fill in any remaining gaps.

Personal preparation

Most of the points in the above section relate to handling administrative arrangements on behalf of the group. Consider, now, your preparation as an individual. What do you need to do to be ready to 'hit the ground running' as soon as the meeting commences?

> ### STOP AND THINK
>
> Instead of immediately thinking about all the positive things you need to do, it might be helpful to begin with some 'reverse brainstorming' as follows:
>
> (a) Assume that you intend to undertake no personal preparation whatsoever. Make a list of all the difficulties you could experience during the meeting itself as a consequence of zero personal preparation.
> (b) Now analyse your list from (a) above and make another one. This time write down all the things you would need to do to prevent the difficulties highlighted on the original list from happening!

How did you get on? Hopefully, the realisation of all the things that could go wrong inspired you to create a robust list of proactive strategies to ensure that they don't! Please take a careful note of the following suggestions and remember to include a customised version of them in your strategy file for each meeting as outlined in Chapter 5.

Read the agenda to acquire an overview of the proceedings: In Chapter 6, it was strongly recommended that the objectives for each item should be included on the agenda. Where this is done, a simple scan of the agenda provides a useful 'snapshot' of the key objectives for the entire meeting.

Read all relevant supporting papers

It is good to be up-to-speed with all the background information relating to each of the agenda items. This will enable you to follow the discussion with greater ease and increase your confidence. If there are numerous papers to read and some of the papers are particularly lengthy, reading them thoroughly may seem to present too great a challenge. However, the effort expended will pay dividends and it may not be necessary to read every word. If the objectives *have* been included on the agenda, then for each item, it may be reasonably straightforward to scan the papers and isolate the key elements that relate to the objectives for that item.

Read the minutes of the last meeting

It is essential to remind yourself of the previous proceedings and the salient issues. This will allow you to create a mental link between the previous meeting and the current topics for discussion.

Undertake additional research if required

If the subject matter is quite complex and/or is unfamiliar to you, it may be beneficial to undertake additional research so that you acquire a greater understanding of the subject.

Check your understanding of technical terms and jargon

This is particularly important if this is a new meeting for you and the subject matter is heavily laden with technical terms. Discuss the issue with the chairperson and then make a list of the relevant terms and their meaning. Make sure that you take it with you to the meeting for reference. Ensure that it is revised and updated as necessary. You may also need to talk to some of the participants to clarify certain terms. It is important that you are proactive in this matter, because in the meeting itself, participants will be unlikely – and probably unwilling – to keep stopping to explain the terms to you!

Determine the layout style for the minutes

If you are minuting a meeting for the first time, it is important to be crystal clear about what is expected in the final minutes. This will then shape your approach to taking the notes. Even if you have the previous minutes to refer to, it is good practice to discuss with the chairperson exactly what is expected in terms of the level of detail, style of writing and presentation.

Meet with the chairperson prior to the meeting

The importance of this cannot be overstated. Ideally, the chairperson and the minute-taker should work as a team and the pre-meeting briefing provides an opportunity to discuss a range of issues in connection with the smooth running of the meeting. This may happen at the meeting itself just prior to commencement. That is better than not at all, but the best approach is to meet in private, well in advance of the actual meeting.

> **ICSA GOOD PRACTICE**
>
> **Relationship with the chairman**
>
> It is generally a good idea for the person minuting the meeting to discuss with the chairman before the meeting any relevant procedural issues and, perhaps most importantly, how they can best support the chairman. This is also an opportunity to give feedback to the chairman on how he or she can best help the minute taker. For example, many company secretaries find it helpful for the chairman to provide a brief summary of the outcome of discussions at the end of each item of business, giving directors the opportunity to agree or suggest amendments to that summary. It is the responsibility of the minute taker to request clarification if there is any doubt as to the outcome of discussions or the conclusion reached.

Meet with participants prior to the meeting

This is beneficial for several reasons. First, it provides an opportunity to seek clarification about issues which you are struggling to understand. By talking with the participant responsible for presenting the 'problematic' item, you will gain the clarification you need and feel far more confident when taking the notes for that item. Ideally, you should try to meet before the day of the meeting so that you have longer to absorb the information. If that is not possible, do try to meet briefly on the day itself. Second, introducing yourself to any new members and to those who are attending for specific items only will help you in remembering their names when the meeting commences. Finally, talking with participants prior to the meeting helps to 'break the ice'. If none or very few of the participants are known to you, introducing yourself to everyone helps convey the fact that you are a fellow professional. This will make you feel more confident and less self-aware.

Be conversant with meeting rules and procedures

Although the chairperson is responsible for conducting the meeting, it is helpful if you are aware of how the meeting should be run. You are then in a better position to assist the chairperson when necessary. For example, you need to understand what the quorum is so that you can keep track of people arriving and leaving and remind the chairperson should the meeting become inquorate.

Prepare yourself physically and mentally

Note taking – particularly at very long meetings – can be mentally exhausting and it is important that you are physically and mentally prepared. Try to get a good night's sleep before minuting a demanding meeting and ensure that on the day you drink plenty of water: you must keep hydrated. It is also a good idea to take a nutritious slow-release energy snack, such as a banana. This is a lot more effective than high-energy soft drinks and too much coffee! Whatever you do, it might be a good idea to use the toilet before the meeting!

Assemble all the necessary materials

You will need the following:

- Notepad or laptop.
- Pen and/or pencil plus spares.
- Highlighter pens.
- The agenda and accompanying paperwork.
- Minutes of the previous meeting.
- Information regarding rules and procedures for the meeting.
- A list of technical terms and their meaning.
- A list of abbreviations, symbols and personalised shorthand phrases for note-taking.
- A watch or small clock to keep track of time.

Ideally, your notepad should be A4 size and spiral bound. This will allow you to record the information for most items without having to turn over too many pages. You can, of course, take a loose-leaf approach if you prefer, but if you do, ensure that all the sheets are numbered. Another alternative is to prepare a note-taking template based on the agenda. This takes the form of an elongated agenda with plenty of white space to record the notes. This can be quite effective, particularly where the agenda indicates the objectives for each item.

You also need to select an appropriate pen to write with. Think back to some of the exams you have sat either at school or university. Do you remember that feeling you experienced an hour or two in, when what you're writing is becoming less and less legible and your little finger feels like it's going to drop off? That is because you're writing at pace and probably gripping a small pen too tightly throughout. When taking the notes at the meeting you need to select a pen of reasonable thickness and ideally with a rubber grip – very handy on a hot and sticky day!

Arrange your writing area

Arrange your writing area so that all your items and materials are assembled before you in a way which facilitates the task. Sit close to the edge of the table, otherwise there is a danger that you will be supporting all the weight of your arm on your wrist. This will make you tired, so move closer so that the majority of your lower arm rests on the table.

Create your own seating plan

In many cases you will know the names of all the participants and any new attendees should be easy to 'target', prior to the start of the meeting. However, if it is a new meeting, or there are new members and other attendees who are unknown to you and you are unable to speak to them all before the meeting, point this out to the chairperson who can then invite everyone to introduce themselves. It is, of course, unlikely, particularly at a new meeting, that you will remember all the names. The solution is to draw a picture of the table and put dots around it to represent the positions where people are sitting. As each person introduces themselves, record the name next to the relevant dot. If the chairperson fails to invite people to introduce themselves, you can always employ the 'clock technique'. Simply allocate a *number* to each person; begin with the person sitting nearest to you, then work your way around the table. You will obviously need to determine the names at some point, but at least it gets you started!

Arrive early

Give yourself plenty of time to meet and greet participants, talk to the chairperson, check the equipment and arrange your own writing area. If you arrive too near the start, you will feel rushed and this may affect your concentration when the meeting begins.

Sit next to the chairperson

You will need to communicate with each other during the meeting so sitting next to the chairperson makes sense. If for some reason you are unable to sit next to the chairperson, make sure that you are not seated too far away; you will need to be in a position to maintain eye contact. If it is a new meeting and someone directs you to a seat which is unsuitable, be assertive and explain why you need to be placed close to the chairperson.

Summary

This chapter has focused on the importance of preparing for the meeting both with regard to general administrative arrangements and personal preparation. As previously mentioned, it will be beneficial to use this information when you are preparing your comprehensive checklists for each meeting as described in Chapter 5. So, with all the preparation having been completed, the next stage of the process is the critical note-taking phase. This is the phase which seems to induce strong feelings of apprehension and concern. Why does this happen and what are the specific techniques which will help to maximise the effectiveness of the note-taking process? These questions will be addressed in Chapter 8.

8
Effective note-taking

The note-taking phase is a little bit like sitting an exam. On the day, you enter the examination room with a sense of trepidation. Your heart beats fast and nervous tension seems to be gaining the upper hand over your usual calm and relaxed disposition! Why do you feel that way? There are possibly three main reasons. First, you know that the couple of hours immediately ahead of you are crucial. This is the set time for the exam – you don't get a second chance. Second, you are concerned that you may not have revised enough. Even though you've tried to cover all the bases, you wonder if there might be one or two questions which could trip you up. Finally, you know that you need a good result. People will judge you on the outcome. Will you make the grade?

Now think of that exam scenario and liken it to the note-taking phase. First, you know that the meeting has been scheduled for a set time. Your window of opportunity to take accurate notes opens when the meeting starts and closes when the meeting ends – you don't get a second chance. Second, you have prepared for the meeting quite diligently but have you prepared enough? Will there be parts of the discussion that you do not understand; could something catch you out? Finally, what if it all goes wrong and the notes are inadequate? What if the draft minutes need major corrections? People may judge your professionalism on the outcome, will you make the grade?

This is an important chapter because if you can master the note-taking phase you will increase in confidence as a minute-taker immeasurably. The *preparation phase* leading up to the meeting may be administratively challenging but it is unlikely to take you out of your comfort zone. Likewise the *minute-writing phase* will challenge your ability to compose effective summaries but you still have the opportunity to edit and re-edit. In the note-taking phase you have to get it right first time and this can make you anxious. This chapter discusses some key principles on how to approach note-taking and the application of a key note-taking technique is examined.

> ### STOP AND THINK
> Think about your own experience as a note-taker and any conversations you may have had with your minute-taking colleagues.
> In your opinion, what is the predominant concern that note-takers have as the meeting commences?

It is probably a safe bet to assume that you came up with this: 'What if I miss something?' Every note-taker knows that the correct information – and enough of it – needs to be captured *at* the meeting to be able to write up the final minutes. This natural concern then leads almost inevitably to the asking of the following question:

> 'Do I have to write everything?'

The question is understandable. If the objective is to not miss out on any vital information, then perhaps '*writing everything*' is the only way to ensure that; a note-taker may reason. If the answer is yes, then the implications for the note-taker are clear: a long, stressful, demanding and totally exhausting experience beckons! Not surprisingly, the above question is one of the most popular that is asked on minute-taking courses. The question delegates on such courses are *really* asking is:

> 'I don't want to have to write everything, so if I don't; what can I do to ensure that no vital information is missed?'

Deciding on an approach to note-taking

Trying to write 'everything' is certainly an *approach* to note-taking, but what does it really achieve? If you decided to take this approach, what would you end up with at the end of the meeting? You would have a set of verbatim-style notes. You would then have to laboriously wade through the script trying to extract the key points. Even if you had highlighted the decisions and actions, you would still struggle in formulating concise summaries of the discussion because your notes would have tracked the *order of the discussion* which may have periodically veered *off* track! There are a number of problems associated with this approach as follows:

- You will become very tired during the meeting itself and this may impair concentration.
- You will be listening for the words not the main thrust of the argument; hence you may fail to get the sense of the discussion.
- The quality of your notes in terms of legibility may decrease as the meeting progresses.
- When you sit down to write the minutes you are faced with a challenging note structuring exercise.
- You will use up valuable time which could be better expended on other tasks.
- In time, you may become very frustrated on a personal level with the minute-taking role.

An alternative approach

Consider an alternative approach. Begin by thinking about your final objective. Chapter 3 drew attention to the ICSA's *Code of Good Boardroom Practice* which stated: 'the minutes should record the decisions taken and provide sufficient background to those decisions'. If this is accepted as a reasonable benchmark then your objective is to produce a clear set of minutes that, for each item discussed, highlight the *key decisions* made, the *reasons* for those decisions and any agreed *actions*. So, three factors are important:

- background
- decisions; and
- actions.

In the final minutes you are going to create a *summary* of the background which led to the decisions. Think for a moment about the 'executive summary' in a written report. This section may be only one or two pages long, but it provides an overview of the entire report (which may be many pages in length). To be effective, the executive summary needs to capture the 'flavour' of the report and to highlight any recommendations. In a similar way, effective minutes aim to capture the 'flavour' of the discussion – the main thrust of the argument – and to highlight any decisions.

If you adopt the 'write everything' approach discussed in the previous section, you have to try to extract the 'flavour' of the discussion from your copious notes taken at the meeting. Instead wouldn't it be better to capture the 'flavour' of the discussion *at* the meeting itself? In order to do this requires a change of approach. Now you need to listen primarily for:

THE MAIN MESSAGE
not
THE WORDS USED

The 'learn' technique

If you aim to capture the main message instead of taking verbatim-style notes, you will acquire a greater understanding of the meeting, your concentration levels will be maintained and you will suffer less from fatigue. In order to do this effectively, the recommendation from the authors of this book is that you adopt the 'LEARN' technique when taking the notes at meetings. The technique is summarised in the box below, following which each point is examined in turn.

LISTEN
EVALUATE
ABBREVIATE
REVIEW
NOTE

Figure 8.1: The LEARN technique

Listen

The 'LEARN' technique is based on a simple principle: 'Listen first, write second'. Now you may think that this is obvious, surely even with the 'write everything' approach you still have to listen first to know what to write? This is true, but there is a difference. When you are trying to write everything, you are almost writing *in parallel* with the speaker; trying to capture the words as soon as possible after they're uttered. Using this approach, you are encouraged to listen for a longer period without taking notes and then, at an appropriate point, to note down the key points of the discussion you have just listened to. There is a more detailed discussion on listening skills in Chapter 12, but in this chapter, the focus is on *why* you are listening and that is primarily to evaluate.

Evaluate

When listening to the discussion your prime purpose is to focus on the main message. So, in evaluative listening, you are trying to figure out what that message is. You need, of course, to listen for the decisions taken and actions agreed, but in terms of the discussion, you need to be selective. What are the points which are necessary to note to enable the summary to be written? You are continually evaluating the 'worth' of the information you are hearing. To do this effectively, you need to be in possession of two things:

- a reasonable understanding of the subject being discussed; and
- a clear understanding of the objectives of the discussion.

With regard to point 1, remember that in Chapter 5 you were encouraged to build a strategy file for each meeting consisting of a checklist of activities tailored to the requirements of the meeting and supporting reference documents to assist you in carrying out those activities. Some of these activities will focus on ensuring that you have a sufficient knowledge base regarding the subjects to be discussed, acquired either through background reading, conversations with participants or both. Note that you are only looking for a reasonable understanding of the subject; just enough so that you feel confident in being able to listen and then identify the key points.

Regarding point 2, do you remember the point made in Chapter 6 about the value of including *the specific objective* for each of the sub-items on the agenda? If you do this you will have a clear understanding of what is to be achieved. This will help to focus your listening and isolate the points relevant to those objectives.

You may feel apprehensive about listening for a period without writing. The following concerns may spring to mind:

1. Will I be able to isolate the key points?
2. Will I forget the key points if I listen for too long without writing?
3. If I listen for a while and then note the key points down, will I miss some of the discussion when I make my notes?

Consider for a moment, the following scenario:

> You have a good friend named Athina whom you haven't seen for nearly ten years. Out of the blue, you receive a phone call; Athina is in town and inviting you to meet up later that evening for a meal. You are excited about meeting her again and really curious about what she has been up to over the past ten years. At the meal, she tells you the following:
>
> - She has lived in Australia for the past five years.
> - She lives on the Gold Coast.
> - She is in the UK for a three-month holiday.
> - She is now married.
> - She has two children: Justin and Jodie, they are twins.
> - She now works as a beautician.
>
> The next day you are talking to a friend at work, who also knew Athina and who is keen to receive an update from you.

How easy will it be for you to provide your friend with an accurate update? Probably very easy indeed! Why? Because you were *interested* in the discussion; you were *relaxed* and *focused* on what was being said. Even if you were talking to your friend *a week later*, you would probably be able to give the same level of detail.

In a sense, you could say that your objective was to find out what your friend had been up to over the past ten years. You would have discussed many things over the course of the evening, but you would have been focused on learning about what had changed in Athina's life. You took no notes, but because you were interested, you were able to absorb the key points and relate them to your friend at work many hours after your meal.

So, applying the learning points from the scenario to the note-taking task, point 1 is not problematic if you know what you are looking for; hence the need to be clear about the objectives. Point 2, is also not a cause for real concern: you are perfectly able to retain the key points after a period of listening if you are both focused on the discussion and reasonably familiar with the subject.

Point 3 is simply a matter of practice. Remember that you are not trying to make copious notes, you are simply summarising parts of the discussion with a few key points (the approach to this is addressed in the next section). Noting down your key points should take no more than a minute. You will need to exercise an element of judgement here and you will benefit from developing your own style. So, there is no definitive rule (e.g. 'you must listen for three minutes and then note down the key points within 30 seconds'). Much will depend on the nature of the discussion and the natural opportunities which present themselves for 'zoning out' and making your notes. Remember that it's very hard to listen meaningfully and write at the same time. So, whatever style you develop, this general approach applies:

- listen for a period of time;
- evaluate the discussion (isolate the main message and identify the key points);
- stop writing at an appropriate point;

- note down your summary; and
- begin listening again and continue the cycle.

Becoming proficient at isolating the main message from a period of discussion will take practice, but as already noted, being reasonably familiar with the subject and understanding the key objectives will facilitate this. However, sometimes the task is made harder by the poor quality of the contributions. Contributions from participants characterised by, for example, waffling or anger can affect your concentration and make it harder to listen. Note the following two examples of contributions made at a meeting.

> **EXAMPLE**
>
> **'Willy Waffle'**
>
> I'm absolutely convinced without any shadow of a doubt whatsoever, that we, as an organising committee need to take the responsibility to arrange for the booking of extra rooms for this year's management conference. There is no doubt in my mind and I believe in the minds of everyone who sits on the organising committee, not to mention the senior management team and, dare I say, a number of the middle managers as well, that there is a significant advantage – dare I say necessity – in acquiring a wide range of views to fully inform us of the many and diverse issues relating to the whole range of management topics relevant to the strategic and operational needs of our business which need to be discussed in the individual workshops and we are obliged, I believe, to ensure that the opportunity for as many of these topics as possible to be explored in greater depth is realised, thus allowing everyone to be more selective about the topics which may interest them the most and which will ultimately contribute to a cohesive management team and thereby place us in the driving seat once more in the ever-changing competitive marketplace in which we operate.

> **EXAMPLE**
>
> **'Norma Nasty'**
>
> It's absolutely ridiculous. I wouldn't mind if it was the first time I'd mentioned it, but it's more like the 101st – quite frankly I'm really struggling to control my temper YEAH – OK? Technology's the way of the future; technology's the answer to all our problems, TECHNOLOGY'S THE MEANING OF LIFE! Come on, surely student mobiles should be switched off in class? You know the other day I got an e-mail from my Head of Department, telling me to come to a meeting – his office is only 10 YARDS FROM MY DESK! It detracts from teaching it detracts from learning, IT'S JUST PLAIN WRONG!

In the first example, a very simple point is being made:

> 'We need to book extra rooms at the conference centre to cover all the break-out sessions.'

Of course most contributors who like to ramble on a bit won't be quite as bad as dear old Willy Waffle! However, listening for the key point from long-winded contributions can present a challenge. In the second example, the key point is also very simple:

> 'Student mobiles should be switched off in class because their use detracts from effective teaching and learning.'

Contributions like this also present a challenge. In this example, Norma is a lecturer in a college. She is obviously frustrated because it would appear that she has raised this issue on a number of previous occasions and nothing has been done about it. However, she is very angry and her entire delivery is emotionally charged. When people are angry it can be very difficult to isolate the main message; there is a natural tendency to focus on the *manner of delivery*. Also, Norma doesn't mention both elements of the key point at the same time. She mentions the mobile point first, but only at the end does she make the linked point about the effect of disturbance on teaching and learning. Also, it *appears* that the point about teaching and learning is related to the issue about the head of department but it is not. Clearly, Norma has an issue with technology; she is not necessarily averse to it, but is furious as to the abuse of it. After the point about the mobiles is made, Norma is distracted and makes a pointed comment about her head of department's use of technology as a poor substitute for face-to-face communication. She then picks up the original point about the mobiles and adds the associated point.

How then can you as the minute-taker, deal with situations like these? Well you cannot control the contribution, but remember the advice in Chapter 5. Part of your preparation for the meeting will involve reflecting on the personalities of the participants and reminding yourself about the contributors who are likely to present the challenges: *forewarned is forearmed*. Of course, this is harder if it is a new or one-off meeting, or if an outburst is unexpected. Someone like Norma for example, might ordinarily be quite placid but be having a bad day! In such situations remember that you can call on the chairperson to clarify points and if appropriate (in the case of a waffler) interrupt and ask for a clarification.

Abbreviate

So, the time has come to take some notes at last! You've listened to the discussion for a period of time, you've evaluated what you've heard and you are clear about the main message. So, what form should your notes take? Because you are only summarising the main message, do your notes still need to be brief or can full sentences be used? Before that question is answered, take a look at the following example of a set of notes. Assume that the note-taker has *not* applied the 'LEARN' technique; but has tried to keep pace with the order of the discussion. To set the scene: A small training company has been working in the United Arab Emirates and has been increasingly spending more time there. As a result, a meeting is called to address accommodation needs.

EXAMPLE

LB	Need to finalise perm accommodation needs 2019 - training needs in Dubai
PD	Accommodation increasingly difficult issue - "I'm fed up" - should be concentrating on training - mind elsewhere. We have 2 choices - flat in Ajman or apartment on Sheikh Zayed Rd - Us - can't organise - affecting my focus
RR	Got to finalise it - can all know what cost is - evenly allocated each month - to PD > 'You expect everything go smooth - Bound be hiccups - Be patient - must explore prices in Sharjah as well + cost of 2 weeks at time - Le Meridian - might get corporate discount.
PD	Not impatient - you - (RR) Procrastinate - more important things
RR	Need to get opinions of others -
IR	Phil's right - has to be choice between Ajman and central Dubai - Sharjah - traffic journey terrible - Emirates Rd - 'unbelievably heavy' - early in the morning
ASK	We can't choose Sharjah - Crowded - high prices, also bad journey - Le Meridian - really worth checking out - lovely decor - restaurants---
	'I agree' (reluctantly)
RR	OK - can check out Le Meridian as well but needs to be quick - I don't
PD	want discuss anymore!
ASK	If everyone OK - will check out rates and deals at all 3? - (LM, Ajman, Sheikh Zayed Rd)
LB	OK - 'everyone are you ok with that? /All OK) - Please then Archana take as an action

STOP AND THINK

Take a few minutes to read through the notes above.

In your opinion, what are the problems with this particular set of notes?

You have probably spotted several problems. First, the note-taker has to follow the order of discussion, but this will not always reflect the logical order of content. For example, the choices proposed by PD at the start are reiterated by IR later on; the problem is that these are not *linked* in any way. Second, *irrelevant* information is included. The note-taker has tried to write too much, so all the petty squabbling and arguing has been noted. Finally, although the decision and action are included, they don't really stand out clearly enough.

EFFECTIVE MINUTE TAKING

Assume now that the note-taker *has* applied the 'LEARN' technique and produces the following set of notes after listening to and evaluating the discussion:

> **E.G. EXAMPLE**
>
> | SPEAKER NAMES | MAIN NOTES | | ACTION |
> |---|---|---|---|
> | LB | **3 Dubai Accommodation**

 Need to finalise accommodation for 2019 | | |
> | PD | - Important to finalise
 - Best choices: Ajman flat or Sz Rd Apartment | ⎫ | |
> | RR | - Need to finalise; better financial planning
 - Need also to explore Sharjah + Le M'n | ⎬ | |
> | IR | - Choice between Ajman & Sz Rd
 - Sharjah traffic bad | ⎭ | |
> | ASK | - Sharjah – bad traffic/prices
 - Keen on Le M'n
 - Check out all 3? | | |
> | LB | - Everyone Ok
 - ASK to pursue | | |
> | | | | ASK |

This looks a lot better! First, the notepaper has been structured more effectively with clearly headed columns. Second, the inclusion of the blank column (third from left) facilitates the linking of associated points. Third, the action point is now standing out clearly. Finally – and most importantly – because the note-taker has listened and evaluated first and fixed the main message and key points firmly in mind, it has been easier to summarise these points using short phrases rather than long sentences.

Of course, this is just an example. You will need to use your judgement regarding exactly how much information you record; this will depend, to an extent, on the nature of the meeting. However, the use of relatively short phrases as summary points, rather than long-winded sentences is recommended.

There are ways of abbreviating your notes even further! This is through the use of personalised shorthand. Use of literal shorthand might seem a good idea to some, but in reality, all that is happening in such cases is that a verbatim record is being made in shorthand form. The notes still have to be summarised. However, if you have this skill, then by all means use it, but apply it just to the key points; don't fall into the trap of writing too much! If you don't possess that skill then you can create your own personalised shorthand abbreviations and symbols. Take a look at the following two boxes:

> **EXAMPLE**   E.G.
>
> **Abbreviations**
>
> | m't | management |
> |---|---|
> | cm'n | communication |
> | m'g | meeting |
> | cte | committee |
> | dept | department |
> | s'y | salary |

> **EXAMPLE**   E.G.
>
> **Symbols**
>
> | © | Confidential |
> |---|---|
> | µ | Unanimous |
> | ☺ | It was agreed |
> | ∴ | Therefore |
> | ∵ | Because |
> | ® | The meeting noted |

The beauty of creating your own abbreviations and symbols is that you can choose whatever you like and no one can criticise you for it! You might be looking at the examples above and questioning their meaning. For example, you can see that some of the symbols are commonly understood in a different way. That's fine; the abbreviations and symbols featured might not carry those meanings for you, but they do for the person who wrote them! You are encouraged to develop a range of personalised shorthand abbreviations and symbols for each of your meetings and include a master list in your strategy file (see Chapter 5). You can add and update periodically. Your shorthand can include common abbreviations which you will use in any meeting but also some very 'meeting specific' ones relating to the subject matter.

So, the use of short phrases and abbreviations can minimise your already succinct notes even further. However, there is a particular problem which needs to be highlighted in relation to long agenda items. Take a look at the following set of notes.

80 EFFECTIVE MINUTE TAKING

E.G. EXAMPLE

THEME	MAIN NOTES	NAMES	AGREED
	<u>4 Staff Dinner & Dance</u>		
Poorly attended	Attendance figure poor over the past 3 years Last year worst of all	AJC	
Reasons why	Why? – - Format is 'old hat' - Midweek date – not practical - Making effort – no incentives - Only staff can attend - Drinks bill 'heavy'	AJC	
How to encourage attendance	Worth coming? Encourage attendance – how? - Need incentive - Able to bring guest Cost central issue – drinks expensive - Wine with meal only! - Need drinks subsidy - Criteria??		
Promoting the event	Promote event? - Email CEO - Managers – staff meeting		
How to organise	Incentives – HR should organise? Liaise hotel? People motivated – move to Friday – sleep off!		
How to encourage attendance	- Subsidy – drinks vouchers? - 8 £4 vs per person		
Promoting the event	Advertise – Social Club Bulletin Board - In-house Magazine - Email from CEO re-iterated		
How to encourage attendance	<u>'free' guest – 5 years' service</u> <u>Drinks subsidy & Friday night also agreed</u>		<u>Agreed</u>
Promoting the event	<u>Email from CEO and in-house mag agreed</u>		<u>Agreed</u>
How to organise	<u>HR organise AJC – report back</u> - Liaise with hotel - Speak to CEO and publishing - Report back next meeting		<u>Agreed</u> <u>ACTION</u>

The example relates to an item about a staff dinner and dance. As note-taking necessarily involves following the order of a discussion rather than the logical order of content, problems can occur when the discussion becomes disjointed and people revisit earlier parts of the debate. This makes the notes harder to structure when you are writing up the final minutes. Where you expect a long period of discussion on an item where this problem would be likely to occur, there is a strategy you can adopt. If you become proficient in applying the 'LEARN' technique, this approach will be straightforward.

Begin by structuring your notepaper a little differently as shown in the example above. The idea is to allocate themes to the various elements of the discussion. Of course, in order to do this, you need to listen first! In the example above, the discussion begins by talking about the trend of poor attendance at the dinner and dance. It then moves on to discuss why this is happening. As you discern the new discussion point, you will probably take the opportunity to pause to record your notes in relation to the point just discussed. When you finish recording your notes, conclude by also allocating a theme – a 'label' – for the part of the discussion which has just concluded and write it in the left-hand margin. In the example, the label is: 'poorly attended'. After the discussion about the 'reasons why' has concluded, allocate another label to sum up that part of the discussion. In the example the label is: 'reasons why'. The discussion then turns to 'how to encourage attendance' and so on. Continue the labelling process until the end of the item. Listen carefully for when you discern that the discussion has reverted back to a former issue, then, at the end of the point, allocate the same label as when that topic was previously discussed.

In the example, you will notice that for the first five parts of the discussion a logical order is followed (i.e. there is a progressive development of the discussion). Then suddenly, someone raises another point about 'how to encourage attendance'. This trend of reverting to former themes continues until the end of the item.

When you look back at your notes, you will see a clear list of themes recorded in the left-hand column, some of which are repeated more than once. As a result, it will be much easier to group 'like with like' when you come to write up the final minutes.

Note-taking templates do not necessarily have to follow the fairly standard structure used in the above examples. More creative approaches can be applied. The 'best' choice will depend to an extent on the length of the agenda item and, of course, your personal preference. One interesting method which tends to work quite well with shorter agenda items is the 'visual recording technique'. An example of this method, using the 'Dubai accommodation 2019' discussion, is shown at the top of the following page.

With this method, the names of the participants are written on the template in relation to the position they are sitting at around the table. Then the various points made by the individual contributors are recorded directly under the name. This works quite well if you are a 'visual' person, the agenda item is not too long and there are not too many participants. Otherwise you may need to record the notes on a sheet of A1!

Another note-taking template that is favoured by some is the spider diagram. The use of the spider diagram is examined in Chapter 9 in connection with structuring the notes before writing up the final minutes, but some people feel comfortable using it as their actual note-taking template. Using the 'staff dinner and dance' example, a spider diagram used for note-taking is shown in Figure 8.2.

82 EFFECTIVE MINUTE TAKING

> **EXAMPLE**
>
> PD
> Important to finalise
> Best choices: Ajman flat; SZ Rd apartment
>
> RR
> Need to finalise; better financial planning
> Need also to explore Sharjah and Le M'n
>
> IR
> Choice between Ajman and SZ Rd
> Sharjah traffic bad
>
> ASK
> Sharjah-bad traffic/prices
> Keen on Le M'n
> Check out all 3?
>
> LB (chairperson)
> Need to finalise accommodation for 2019
> Everyone OK
> ASK to pursue
>
> ACTION: ASK

Poorly attended
- Old format
- Staff only
- Mid-week date bad
- Costly drinks
- No incentive

How to encourage endurance
- Move to a Friday
- Drink vouchers (8 @ £4.00 pp)
- 'Free' guest if five years plus service

Promoting the event
- Email CEO
- In-house magazine
- Staff meetings
- Social Club bulletin board

How to organise
- HR (AJC)
  - Hotel
  - CEO/Publishing
  - Report next meeting

STAFF DINNER & DANCE

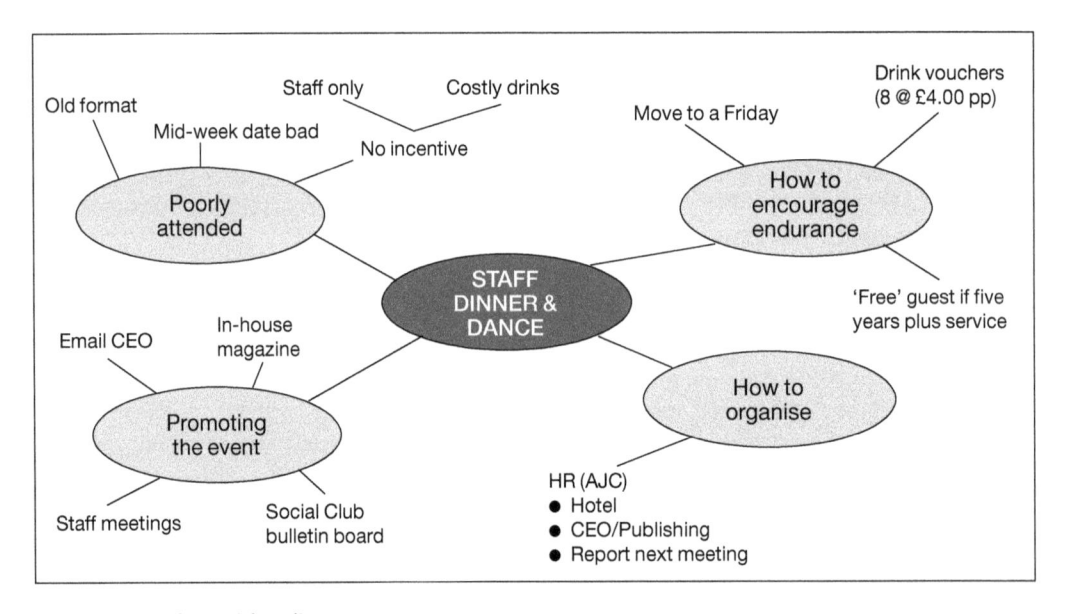

Figure 8.2: The spider diagram

The main topic is written in the centre of the page and circled. Themes are then added and circled as the discussion progresses with sub-points relating to the themes being 'attached' by lines linking to the circles.

If you feel comfortable with the spider diagram (SD) there is one notable advantage over the left-hand margin (LHM) technique discussed previously in this section. With the LHM technique, you end up with a clear list of themes, but some of the labels are repeated because the notes naturally follow the order of discussion. This means that you still have to group together the various points under each theme (if discussed out of the logical order) when you start to write up the final minutes. However, with the SD technique it is different. Once the theme is established, all points relating to that theme (at whatever stage during the discussion they are made) can simply be linked directly to the circle. This means that at the end of the meeting, your information is already grouped.

So, there are a number of options in terms of template choice. Some people, for example, simply create a template from the agenda and allow extra white space between each listed item. You may decide to employ several different methods at the same meeting depending on the length and nature of the items. That is perfectly acceptable; however, think about how your notebook is structured. If you are using blank sheets of A4 then fine, but if you use primarily pre-prepared structured layouts (ruled and annotated) then ensure you incorporate some blank pages if you wish to employ diagrammatic techniques for some of items. In addition, make sure that you remember to write the number and heading of the agenda items as you go along.

Whatever method you choose, there is a key point to remember: You need to apply the 'LEARN' technique. So far, the first three elements of the technique have been addressed in detail. The final two elements are quite straightforward, but no less important.

Review and note

The first thing you probably want to do as soon as the meeting is finished is to get as far away from the meeting room as possible! You must resist that impulse because there is still work to do. You need to take a few minutes to review your notes and then if necessary, to note down any corrections or additional points. Note the following reminders:

- Take a few minutes to read over your notes.
- Check your notes for any adjustments:
    - Do the notes make sense?
    - Are any points illegible?
    - Are any of the phrases or words unclear?
    - Does anything appear to be missing?
- For each agenda item, check that all the decisions and actions are clearly recorded (underline or use a highlighter pen).

For example, if you look back at the spider diagram for the staff dinner and dance item, you will note that there are some points missing. Although it can probably be inferred from the 'how to organise' notes, the two promotional methods chosen should be highlighted ('promoting the event'). Also, although it's fairly clear that AJC from HR will be taking the actions, this should be explicit in the notes. These seem like small things but they can make a difference, particularly if the minutes are not going to be written up immediately following the meeting.

If you require clarification on any points, either from the chairperson or some of the participants, ensure that you speak with them immediately after the meeting and make a note of the clarification. Make a note of it straightaway.

Also make a note if you need to follow anything up. For example, has a participant promised to provide you with a summary of a verbal report? If so, ensure that you agree the arrangements for this because you will need the summary for the final minutes.

ICSA GOOD PRACTICE

Retention of notes

It is usual practice for company secretaries to keep their written notes of board meetings until the final version of the minutes are formally approved at a subsequent board meeting.

Some company secretaries keep their written notes indefinitely but it should be clearly understood that any such notes could be 'discoverable' or disclosable in the context of any future litigation.

On balance we recommend that the notes should be retained until the minutes are approved, but then promptly destroyed. The risks associated with disclosure or discovery requirements outweigh the benefits.

Summary

This chapter has addressed the challenges posed by the anxiety-inducing note-taking phase and has provided a framework for effective note-taking in the form of the 'LEARN' technique. Various note-taking templates have also been discussed including the use of visual recording and spider diagrams. The examples shown in the chapter have illustrated how the notes can be produced using the minimum of detail. Remember they are only examples: you must make a judgement as to how much detail to include in your own notes. However, always keep in mind the guiding principle 'listen first, write second'.

The notes form the foundation from which the final minutes will be prepared. However, before that can happen, they need to be structured appropriately. This topic is addressed in Chapter 9.

9
Transforming notes into minutes

Are you a fan of Superman? If you are, no doubt you are always thrilled to observe the part when by means of a spectacular transformation, the mild-mannered Clark Kent suddenly turns into the Man of Steel! If only all transformations were as simple! Wouldn't it be wonderful to observe, as if by magic, your notes from the meeting suddenly transform into the perfect set of final minutes?

Well, the good news is that your notes *will* transform into the perfect set of final minutes; the bad news is that it's only going to happen with a lot of hard work! The purpose of this chapter is to discuss what needs to happen from the point that you walk out of the meeting room up to the point that you sit down to write the final minutes. The following areas will be discussed:

- techniques for streamlining your notes in preparation for writing the minutes
- choosing the appropriate style of minutes
- writing style
- avoiding errors in writing
- developing your minute-writing toolkit:
  – checklist of useful words
  – checklist of useful phrases
  – reference material
  – templates.

Techniques for streamlining the notes

If you apply the advice and tips in Chapter 8, your notes will already be in an easy-to-read streamlined form when you sit down to write the minutes. Also, you will have spent a few minutes tidying-up your notes and checking for any illegibility or unclear points at the end of the meeting. So, as you sit down to write, you can be confident that the task ahead of you – although demanding – will not be too onerous!

In front of you will be your A4 bound notepad (or loose-leaf numbered papers) containing all your notes. Your notes may be in different formats depending on the blend of techniques you have used. For example, you may have used a standard note-taking template for some items and a spider diagram for others. The amount of streamlining required before you begin to write will depend, to some extent, on the techniques you used.

86 EFFECTIVE MINUTE TAKING

Example 1

First of all, consider the example of the notes regarding the staff dinner and dance agenda item discussed in Chapter 8. The notes from the meeting are shown below:

E.G. EXAMPLE

THEME	MAIN NOTES	NAMES	AGREED
	4 Staff Dinner & Dance		
Poorly attended	Attendance figure poor over the past 3 years Last year worst of all	AJC	
Reasons why	Why? – - Format is 'old hat' - Midweek date – not practical - Making effort – no incentives - Only staff can attend - Drinks bill 'heavy'	AJC	
How to encourage attendance	Worth coming? Encourage attendance – how? - Need incentive - Able to bring guest Cost central issue – drinks expensive - Wine with meal only! - Need drinks subsidy - Criteria??		
Promoting the event	Promote event? - Email CEO - Managers – staff meeting		
How to organise	Incentives – HR should organise? Liaise hotel? People motivated – move to Friday – sleep off!		
How to encourage attendance	- Subsidy – drinks vouchers? - 8 £4 Vs per person		
Promoting the event	Advertise – Social Club Bulletin Board - In-house Magazine - Email from CEO re-iterated		
How to encourage attendance	'free' guest – 5 years' service Drinks subsidy & Friday night also agreed		Agreed
Promoting the event	Email from CEO and in-house mag agreed		Agreed
How to organise	HR organise AJC – report back - Liaise with hotel - Speak to CEO and publishing - Report back next meeting		Agreed ACTION

Your notes from the meeting will naturally follow the order of the discussion for each agenda item. Therefore, whenever you seek to develop a set of minutes from the notes you have taken in the meeting, there are always three things that you need to do for each item:

- make a list of the key points including decisions and actions;
- group the points together in a logical order; and
- write up the minute.

The greater the level of detail recorded in your notes, the greater the level of difficulty in undertaking these three tasks. Some people go directly into writing the minute, picking points out of the notes as they see fit. This is one way of doing it, but it usually results in significant editing and re-editing.

As noted in the previous chapter, the example above relates to a long agenda item in which the discussion follows a logical sequence for a while before losing its 'shape' when the order of discussion becomes disjointed. In this case the margin on the left-hand side was used to summarise elements of the discussion under key themes. So, if you were now looking to write the minute from this set of notes, you would already have undertaken much of the work! The approach would be as follows:

- Determine the logical order of content based on themes from the margin on the left. In this case that would be:
  - trend of poor attendance for the staff dinner and dance;
  - the reasons why;
  - suggestions for encouraging attendance;
  - suggestions for promoting the event; and
  - organisational arrangements.
- Using a highlighter pen, colour code each of the theme descriptors in the margin. Use a different colour for each theme.
- Begin writing the minute in the logical order of content, drawing in the information from the notes relating to each theme to the level of detail required. Because the themes are highlighted, it will be easier to identify the key points from the notes and group the information together as you are writing. However, if you wanted to, you could summarise the key points first and then move on to write the minute. An example is given below for the theme: Suggestions for promoting the event:

Suggestions for promoting the event
Discussion on various options
    Four proposed:

- An e-mail from the CEO to all staff – *agreed*.
- A short article in the in-house magazine – *agreed*.
- Message on Social Club Bulletin Board.
- Briefing by manager at staff meeting.

88 EFFECTIVE MINUTE TAKING

If you choose to, you could undertake one extra stage of streamlining before writing up the minute: extract the key points from your notes and transfer them into a spider diagram as shown below.

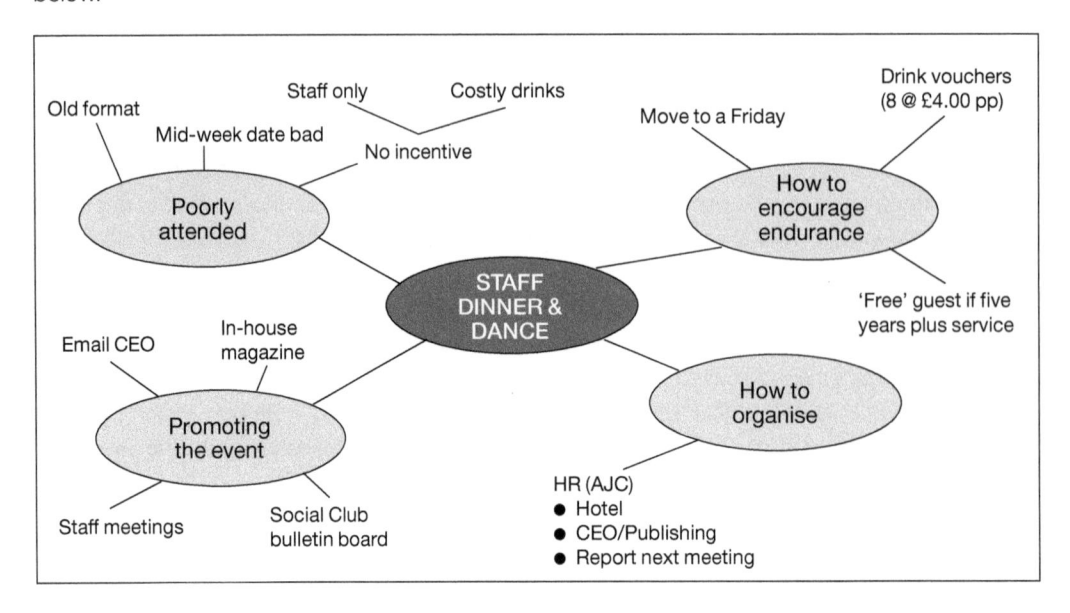

```
                Staff only    Costly drinks                           Drink vouchers
    Old format                                                        (8 @ £4.00 pp)
                Mid-week date bad              Move to a Friday
                              No incentive
              ┌──────────┐                            ┌──────────┐
              │  Poorly  │                            │  How to  │
              │ attended │                            │encourage │
              └──────────┘                            │endurance │
                              ┌──────────┐            └──────────┘
                              │  STAFF   │
                              │ DINNER & │                    'Free' guest if five
                              │  DANCE   │                    years plus service
                 In-house     └──────────┘
    Email CEO    magazine
                                            ┌──────────┐
              ┌──────────┐                  │  How to  │
              │Promoting │                  │ organise │
              │the event │                  └──────────┘
              └──────────┘
                                        HR (AJC)
                            Social Club  ● Hotel
    Staff meetings          bulletin board ● CEO/Publishing
                                        ● Report next meeting
```

The key points are summarised very clearly and it is quite easy to write your minute from the information contained in the diagram. Some people may consider this an unnecessary step which only serves to elongate the process. Much depends on your own style and preferred approach, but it is a useful technique to keep in mind, particularly when dealing with long agenda items, because it provides that extra degree of clarity before you begin writing the minute. The example above would allow you to write a reasonably detailed minute because it includes all four options for promoting the event, not just the two that were chosen. It also provides some background detail regarding the reasons for poor attendance.

EXERCISE

Using a piece of notepaper, please take a few minutes to complete the following exercise:

- Study the spider diagram summary of the staff dinner and dance agenda item. From the information given, **write the minute** in respect of the item
- In terms of the level of detail, you have a choice. You can produce a shorter minute which (a) just introduces the fact that attendance has been poor and therefore there is a need to address it (no need to supply the reasons) and (b) describes only the promotional activities agreed (not all four options). Alternatively, you can produce a slightly longer version using most of the information in the diagram.

If you attempted the exercise before reading on, how long did it take? You were probably able to complete the exercise quite quickly because the spider diagram provides a clear visual 'snapshot'. Even if you choose to add a little extra detail from the notes, it is a good way to mentally capture the structure of your minute. An example of the completed exercise is shown below:

> EXERCISE
>
> AJC informed the meeting that attendance figures for the staff dinner and dance had been poor over the past three years with last year being the most poorly attended of the three. Discussion took place regarding ways to stimulate interest for the forthcoming event. It was agreed that the event would now be moved to a Friday, each member of staff would be given eight free drinks vouchers (each one £4 in value) and all staff with five years' service or more would be allowed to bring a guest for free. With regard to pre-event promotion, it was agreed that a short article would appear in the next in-house magazine and that an e-mail to all staff would be sent by the CEO. It was agreed that AJC would contact the hotel regarding the booking arrangements, speak with the CEO and the publishing department regarding the promotion and report back to the group at the next meeting.
>
> ACTION: AJC

If you completed the exercise, your minute may look very different from the example given above in terms of style. Everyone will have their own style and will emphasise the key points in a different way. Some points about the style of minutes and writing style are made further on in the chapter but the key point to note from the exercise is how straightforward it is to write up the final minute when the notes are structured beforehand.

The use of the left hand margin to create a 'themed identifier' for elements of the discussion makes the structuring process far easier; so its use during the meeting is recommended, particularly for 'meaty' agenda items.

Example 2

Example 2 looks again at the 'Dubai accommodation' example featured in Chapter 8. The notes are reproduced opposite.

As before, the three essential tasks need to be performed:

- make a list of the key points including decisions and actions;
- group the points together in a logical order; and
- write up the minute.

This example illustrates the benefit of only recording the key points in the notes and using short phrases rather than longer sentences to record the information. In this case, even though a degree of grouping is required, the minute could probably be written directly from the notes page, with points 1 and 2 above being performed mentally. Also, there would be no need to produce a spider diagram to achieve an extra degree of clarity. A possible wording for the minute is shown opposite:

EFFECTIVE MINUTE TAKING

E.G. EXAMPLE

SPEAKER NAMES	MAIN NOTES		ACTION
	<u>3 Dubai Accommodation</u>		
LB	Need to finalise accommodation for 2019		
PD	- Important to finalise - Best choices: <u>Ajman</u> flat or <u>Sz Rd</u> Apartment	⎫	
RR	- Need to finalise; better financial planning - Need also to explore <u>Sharjah</u> + <u>Le M'n</u>	⎬	
IR	- Choice between <u>Ajman</u> & <u>Sz Rd</u> - Sharjah traffic bad	⎭	
ASK	- Sharjah – bad traffic/prices - Keen on <u>Le M'n</u> - Check out all 3?		
LB	- Everyone Ok - ASK to pursue		
			<u>ASK</u>

E.G. EXAMPLE

The board discussed the importance of finalising the accommodation requirements for 2019. Four possibilities were proposed: accommodation options in Sharjah, a flat in Ajman, an apartment on Sheikh Zayed Road and the block-booking of Le Meridien. It was agreed that ASK would investigate the latter three options and report back at the next meeting.

ACTION: ASK

Example 3

The approach to structuring is similar for the visual recording method. The notes are reproduced below.

> **EXAMPLE**
>
> PD
> Important to finalise
> Best choices: Ajman flat; SZ Rd apartment
>
> RR
> Need to finalise; better financial planning
> Need also to explore Sharjah and Le M'n
>
> IR
> Choice between Ajman and SZ Rd
> Sharjah traffic bad
>
> ASK
> Sharjah-bad traffic/prices
> Keen on Le M'n
> Check out all 3?
>
> LB (chairperson)
> Need to finalise accommodation for 2019
> Everyone OK
> ASK to pursue
>
> ACTION: ASK

Because this method works quite well for relatively short agenda items, it should again be easy enough to write the minutes straight from the notes. There is one point to note however. In the 'standard' approach to note-taking (see Example 2) the order of discussion is followed faithfully: 'LB' opened the discussion and closed it, as can be seen clearly from the notes. With the visual recording method, all comments are grouped together (chronologically) under the individual's name. When writing up the minute, it is important to keep this point in mind.

Other recording methods

Some people may employ the spider diagram as a direct note-taking tool. If you choose this method you will have some advantages at the write-up stage because you will already have a number of points grouped around a series of key themes with decisions and actions highlighted. So, begin by making a list of the order of key points and then from there, it should be reasonably straightforward to write up the minute from the notes. Of course, there may be a need to *consolidate* points for the minutes, so you may need to go through first and eliminate any irrelevant parts and group together various other parts. You can achieve this by crossing out some elements and using arrows to link others.

Summary of the streamlining process

With regard to the writing of the final minutes, the objective for you as a minute-taker is to remove as much stress from the process as possible, so you can focus your concentration on creating a clear summary of the proceedings. The key point to remember is that being effective during the note-taking phase is essential. A clear yet concise set of notes which captures the key points, decisions and actions will greatly reduce the work you need to do in terms of structuring the notes, leaving you with at least some energy for the writing up!

Choosing the appropriate style of minutes

There is no universally accepted style for minutes because organisational and meeting requirements vary considerably. Some groups will want the 'bare bones' of the discussion with the emphasis on decisions and actions. Others will want the decisions and actions to be 'framed' by supporting narrative. Some committees insist on a considerable level of detail (e.g. a joint consultative committee where staff and management employees meet together on a regular basis) and may require a reasonably detailed set of minutes to demonstrate the 'flavour' of the key issues discussed and the reasons behind any decisions taken.

As a minute-taker, you may be required to adapt to a variety of styles, but a set of minutes is still a summary of the proceedings and the art of good minute writing involves the ability to summarise. Some groups favour 'verbatim-style' minutes, where the order of discussion is emphasised. This tends to result in a fragmented record of events so; even here there may be a need to group some information together in the form of summaries. It is bad minute-writing practice to continually attribute comments to individuals (exactly who said what and when), and this can be a tendency if the order of discussion rather than the logical order of content is emphasised. More is said about this and the use of participant names in the next chapter.

Writing style

Traditionally, minutes are written using the passive, past tense. Some people advocate a more active style of writing because they argue that use of the passive voice makes the minutes dull and lifeless, devoid of character and generally uninteresting to read. However, it should be remembered that the purpose of minutes is not to entertain; they are intended to constitute an *objective* record of the meeting. There is no place in formal minutes for subjective interpretations; this is why employing the passive voice, is still the generally accepted approach to minute writing. This traditional style aids objectivity because it is more impersonal, it 'strips-out' emotions and personal feelings. So, minutes should be written using the passive voice and in the third person (e.g. he, she, it, the Head of Marketing). The example opposite shows the difference between the active voice and the passive voice:

Active
The IT Director told the board all about the significant progress on the revised implementation plan.

Passive
It was noted that significant progress had been made on the revised implementation plan.

Never use personal pronouns such as: I, we, me, my, you, your, our, us, in the writing of formal minutes. Look at the two phrases below:

> It was agreed that, as a board of directors, we need to be more proactive in pursuing contractual opportunities.

> It was agreed that the board of directors needed to be more proactive in pursuing contractual opportunities.

The second example would be more in keeping with the style of formal minutes.

Care also needs to be exercised regarding the issue of *reported speech*. Take a look at the following two examples:

> '"I disagree with the style of the proposal", said the Head of Marketing.'

> The Head of Marketing said that he disagreed with the style of the proposal.

Again, the second example illustrates the more appropriate style. In minute writing you are not aiming to include direct quotes from people; you are *reporting* what they say.

Use of the passive voice is traditional in minute writing, but there are easy mistakes to make. For example, note the following:

> The head of finance summarised the key points from the report.

> The key points from the report were summarised by the head of finance.

The difference is subtle, but the second option would be the more correct approach. Consider another example:

> It was decided to hold the interviews in the board room.

> It was decided that the interviews would be held in the board room.

At first glance, the first example appears to be correct, but the use of the word 'that' is missing. The second example is the correct approach. The problem for you as the minute-taker is that in the meeting itself, people will not be conversing using the passive voice! So, you always have to think carefully about how the minutes should read. For example, if the finance director says in the meeting: '… all the candidates have been very professional', you have to think how to report that using the passive voice. So, your actual wording in the minutes would probably read more like this:

> '… all the candidates had been very professional'.

ICSA GOOD PRACTICE

Reported speech

Our research has shown that the use of reported, rather than direct, speech is still the overwhelming majority practice. It provides consistently clear, concise minutes which avoid ambiguity. Some organisations do find it an old-fashioned or overly formal style, but our recommendation is to retain it unless there is good reason not to do so.

Summarising

As already noted, the ability to summarise is a key skill for minute-writers. Applying the guidelines in this chapter on the structuring of notes will help you achieve this more easily. When summarising, you are building everything around the key points; specifically the decisions and actions. In this way, you maintain the 'shape' of the meeting. All your narrative should be built around these key points. This means that you are not trying to capture the order of the discussion or give a detailed account of what everyone has said. Rather, you are grouping together elements of the discussion in a logical order, linked to the key points. It is not necessary to give a 'blow-by-blow' account of the discussion, just keep the key points to the fore. So effective summarising will include phrases which consolidate elements of the discussion such as: 'following a detailed discussion' and 'a discussion took place'. This issue is re-emphasised in the following chapter when discussing the recording of decisions and actions.

Also, try to be *fluent* in your style of writing. In your notes you will have used bullet points to capture key ideas, but now, when writing, you need to express those ideas in sentences. Avoid the habit of using very short sentences because your style will appear 'jagged' and will be hard to read. Indeed, sometimes your sentences will have to be quite long because you are aiming to summarise elements of the discussion.

TRANSFORMING NOTES INTO MINUTES

Minute-taking is an art and you are the artist, so develop your own style! The following examples show various ways of writing parts of the discussion sections. They are just examples. Hopefully, they will give you some ideas as you continue to develop your own approach. Some of the examples are quite brief, others are a little longer, but remember that you may face different requirements regarding the level of detail depending on the nature of the meetings you minute.

EXAMPLE 1

The secretary reported that she had investigated the requirements of the university's ethical approval policy and tabled a brief summary sheet of the action she felt was necessary for the department to take in order to comply with the requirements.

EXAMPLE 2

These views were echoed by the Director of Administration who suggested that staff representatives should not look upon the managers' consultative committee as a threat, but rather as a logical development of the communication processes within the organisation and as an enhancement to existing consultative machinery.

EXAMPLE 3

Concern was expressed that current levels of service in the membership division appeared to be falling short of meeting the agreed standards. Following a detailed discussion, the meeting noted that within the next quarter, the management committee would be undertaking an in-depth review of performance with regard to service level agreements, in each of the five divisions

EXAMPLE 4

Regarding selling prices, Jim Bancroft informed the meeting that ABC Caterers were in the process of preparing specific proposals for approval, with a proposed implementation date of 4 December 2018. The proposals would be fully discussed by the staff restaurant liaison committee on 15 November. The prices of main dishes (such as meat and fish) would not be affected as they were flexi-priced (i.e. priced each day by reference to the actual cost of the raw materials being used). However, prices of other items such as vegetables, sandwiches, salads, a la carte items and drinks were not flexi-priced and had not been reviewed since September 2015; these prices were therefore overdue for review. Average retail price inflation during this

> **EXAMPLE continued**
>
> time had been approximately 3.5%; however some food prices had risen much more than that and some less. The selling price increase (and reductions) would reflect primarily the increase or reduction in the cost of the actual raw materials concerned and also, to some extent, the net cost purchasing policy and the fact that ABC Caterers had previously retained variable rates of discount (10% discount on some items and 0% on others). In future, selling prices (other than flexi-prices) would be reviewed quarterly by the restaurant liaison committee with any increases being applicable in May, August, November (and February) in each year.

Example 1 illustrates a succinct approach with the key point being developed in one sentence. Example 2 illustrates the reporting of what was said on a particular issue; again in one sentence. Example 3 illustrates a summarising technique: the use of a key phrase; in this case: 'Following a detailed discussion'. Example 4 features a section from the recording of a very detailed discussion on a particular topic. This level of detail will not be required for most of the meetings you minute, but it is important to take note of the style, particularly if you are asked to take the minutes at, for example, a joint consultative committee where there may be a requirement for a more detailed account of events.

Avoiding errors in writing

In Chapter 10, there is a section on the importance of proofreading. Of course, the simpler you make this task for yourself the better: aim to get it right first time! No one is perfect, that's true and even experienced minute-takers make mistakes. However, much can be avoided by just taking that extra bit of care when writing. For example, read the following phrase:

> 'Rob Robson says Phil Davis is an idiot.'

Who is the idiot? Phil Davis of course. Why? Because Rob Robson says so! Look again:

> 'Rob Robson, says Phil Davis, is an idiot.'

Who is the idiot now? Rob Robson of course. Why? Because Phil Davis says so!

The insertion of just two small commas has created a 100% change in meaning! So, be careful with punctuation, although you probably won't make a mistake quite like the example above, the correct emphasis can sometimes be lost due to inappropriate punctuation. One common mistake relates to the use of its and it's. The simple rule is to replace it's with it is and see if it still makes sense. For example, note the following phrase:

> It's time for a review of the recruitment policy

When replaced with *it is*, it reads:

> It is time for a review of the recruitment policy

This makes sense, so the use of *it's* makes sense. Now take a look at this example:

> It's engine was malfunctioning

When replaced with *it is*, it reads:

> It is engine was malfunctioning

This doesn't make sense, so in this case the use of *its* would be correct.

Also, be very careful with your spelling and remember that 'spell check' does not necessarily mean 'safe check'! Words may be *spelt* correctly, but *applied* incorrectly. For example, is the head of a college called a principle? No, the correct word is principal. Imagine that you were recording a point about office supplies and you referred to 'the stationary requirements'. That would be fine if you were trying to make the point that the requirements were not moving! Such errors might seem small, but they can reduce the professional appearance of your minutes, so take extra care.

Developing your minute-writing toolkit

When you begin to write you are constantly making choices about the correct words and phrases to use. The following two tables provide some examples for you. Again, they are just ideas; feel free to add to the lists and create your own! In the checklist of useful phrases, for the sake of the example, the fictitious initials 'AJC' are used to denote the participant's name.

CHECKLIST

Checklist of useful words

acceptable	constituents	in advance	proposed
acceptance	constituted	including	provided
accepted	consultation	increase	provisions
acknowledgement	contents	in-depth	pursued
added	context	indicated	raised
additional	contribution	influence	received
addressed	criteria	informed	recognised
advantaged	current	initiative	recommended
advised	deadline	instructed	recorded
agreed	debate	interest	referred
aimed	decided	introduced	regarding
alternatives	declared	investigated	regulation
amendments	decrease	issues	reinforced
analysis	deferred	item	reiterated
announced	delegated	judged	reminded
approach	delivering	latest	report
approved	demonstrated	likelihood	reported
arrangements	demonstrating	maintain	representatives
assist	desirability	members	represented
assurance	development	mitigate	requested
attached	differences	monitor	requirements
background	disadvantaged	nominated	resolved
believed	disagreed	noted	responded
benefits	discriminatory	notified	response
breached	discussed	obstacles	review
chairperson	dissent	opportunity	revised
challenge	drawbacks	options	revisions
circulated	effective	outlined	selected
clarification	eligibility	overcome	significant
clarified	emphasised	overview	specific
commencement	enhancement	papers	stakeholders
committed to	equitable	pointed out	stated
comply	establishing	policy	strategy
concerning	estimated	possibility	subject to
concerns	examined	presented	substantive
concluded	explained	previous	suggested
conditional	expressed	previously	summarised
confidential	further	principal	tabled
confirmation	highlighted	principle	trends
confirmed	impact on	probability	undertook
congratulated	implementation	process	updated
consensus	implications	progress	value
consequence	important	prompted	welcomed
consider	imposed	proposals	

CHECKLIST

Checklist of useful phrases

A report from AJC recommending that	In a detailed discussion
After discussion it was resolved that	In connection with
AJC advised that	In response to a question from
AJC advised the committee	In response to questions raised by
AJC commenced his presentation by	In response to suggestions made by
AJC commented that	It was agreed
AJC concluded his report by	It was decided
AJC concluded the discussion by	It was noted
AJC drew attention to	It was proposed that
AJC drew the board's attention to	It was resolved that
AJC emphasised that	Reporting on her recent visit to
AJC explained that	The board agreed
AJC expressed concern that	The board approved the
AJC further advised that	The board congratulated
AJC informed the meeting	The board recognised that
AJC introduced the paper	The Board requested
AJC made reference to the discussions	The board welcomed the initiative
AJC made reference to the question raised by	The chairperson referred to
AJC made the point that	The chairperson reminded board members
AJC outlined the	The chairperson requested an update
AJC pointed out that	The chairperson welcomed
AJC raised the issue of	The committee believed that it was important
AJC read a prepared statement to the meeting as follows	The committee noted
AJC requested that	The committee was asked to note
AJC requested that in future	The committee was assured that
AJC responded that	The committee was informed that
AJC stressed the need for	The company secretary was requested
AJC suggested that	The following points were noted
AJC then summarised the	The meeting discussed
AJC undertook to	The meeting noted
AJC updated members	The secretary confirmed that
AJC, making reference to	The secretary reported that
Discussion took place	The secretary was instructed to
Following further discussion it was agreed that	There was discussion about
Following on from the discussions relating to	With regard to the situation in

Reference material

When you begin writing, ensure that you have all the necessary reference material you need in front of you. Note the following checklist:

- Your original notes from the meeting.
- Your structured notes.
- The minutes of the previous meeting.
- Your checklist of useful words.
- Your checklist of useful phrases.
- The list denoting the meanings of all the abbreviations, symbols and personalised shorthand phrases used in the note-taking process.
- All the papers that were circulated with the agenda.
- Any papers circulated at the meeting.
- Any notes regarding verbal reports given at the meeting.
- Any other information which you deem to be helpful.

Templates

You will find it beneficial to *prepare a master template* for each of the meetings you minute. This will give you a clearly defined structure and layout at the outset. All the correct headings will be in place and some of the information will remain the same. You will need to make adjustments and updates and you will still have to create your summary of the discussion for each of the agenda items, but having the structure in place will make you feel that you've made some progress even before you start! Remember to include the master template in your strategy file for each meeting.

Summary

This chapter has focused on an analysis of techniques for streamlining your notes in preparation for the writing of the minutes. Tips have been given regarding writing style and how to avoid some of the more common errors in minute writing. You have been encouraged to assemble your own minute-writing toolkit consisting of checklists of useful words and phrases, all reference material relevant to the writing process and your master template.

In the following chapter, the structure of the minutes will be examined in greater detail, including the information required under each heading, suggestions for the recording of decisions and actions and the use of numbering systems.

10
Structure, style and layout

So, the nerve-wracking part is over; you've taken the notes and thought about how you're going to transform them into minutes; you have your list of useful words, terms and phrases in front of you: the time has arrived to write up the final minutes!

This phase presents a different kind of challenge to the note-taking stage, but it is no less daunting, particularly for new and inexperienced minute-takers. What format should be followed? What should the headings be? What needs to be included under each heading? What numbering system is required? How should background discussion, decisions and actions be recorded? All these factors need to be taken into account when writing up the final minutes.

There is no universally accepted format for the minutes. Organisations have their own rules regarding structure, style and layout. As a result, practice differs widely between different organisations and even within organisations; there can be a variety of layout styles and different approaches to what is recorded and in how much detail. For example, with regard to companies, Andrew Hamer in the *ICSA Meetings and Minutes Handbook* states:

Many different styles of presentations may be adopted provided that the minutes include the following basic elements:

- name of the company;
- type of meeting (e.g. annual general meeting or audit committee);
- place where the meeting was held;
- day of the meeting (optional);
- date of the meeting;
- time of the meeting (optional);
- names and/or numbers present;
- record of the proceedings; and
- chairman's signature.

The majority of the elements above relate to information that will appear on the front page of the minutes and will be generally applicable to most types of organisation. However, note the penultimate point: 'record of the proceedings'. The core text of the minutes will be devoted to this and the contents will necessarily vary depending on the organisation and type of meeting being held. Issues regarding structure, layout, style and the level of detail required, will be governed by the rules of the organisation and/or accepted practice which may have evolved over time. It is important, therefore, to fully acquaint yourself with what is required for each of the meetings you minute. If you have some power to influence these factors, and you feel after reading this chapter that some positive adjustments could be made in the interests of best practice, then be proactive!

Notwithstanding the wide variations in style and layout; in terms of *structure* there is a traditional and generally accepted approach and this is shown below.

> **EXAMPLE**
>
> **Structure of the minutes**
>
> - Heading
> - Listing of attendees
> - Apologies for absence
> - Declarations of Interest
> - Minutes of the previous meeting
> - Matters arising
> - Main agenda items
> - Any other business
> - Date of next meeting

With reference to the generic framework above, the purpose of this chapter is to provide – in respect of each of the headings above – the following:

- The purpose of the item
- The information that needs to be recorded
- Examples of wording and layout.

The chapter concludes with a discussion regarding numbering systems and provides some examples of various approaches.

The heading

There are a number of important details which need to be included on the first page of the minutes. Requirements for companies were listed in the introductory section and these requirements are similar for most organisations. Useful recommendations and guidelines have also been produced by the Charity Commission (e.g. these include the need to record the name of the person chairing the meeting and, not only the names of those present, but the capacity in which they attended). Minutes provide an evidential record for legal purposes so it is essential that all information is recorded accurately. For example, if the time of the meeting is recorded, this should be the *actual* time the meeting commenced. Take the situation where two meetings are held and the business conducted at the second meeting is conditional upon approval being obtained at the first. In such a case, the recording of the actual time will provide evidence that one meeting took place before the other.

STRUCTURE, STYLE AND LAYOUT

Layout practices in terms of the heading vary considerably and much depends on the type of meeting and, of course, the accepted conventions rules and guidelines. It is usually a good idea to maintain the style used in the agenda. Examples of layout styles for different types of meetings are shown below.

> **EXAMPLE**
>
> TMF TRAINING LIMITED
>
> Minutes of a board meeting held at 47 Rathbone Court on 18 September 2018 at 10.30 am.

> **EXAMPLE**
>
> TMF TRAINING LIMITED
>
> Minutes of a
> board meeting held on 18 September 2018
> at 47 Rathbone Court at 10.30 am.

> **EXAMPLE**
>
> TMF TRAINING LIMITED
>
> Minutes of a meeting of the Board
> held on 18 September 2018 commencing at 10.30 am
> in the King's Suite, 47 Rathbone Court, London NW1 7JB

> **EXAMPLE**
>
> <u>MINUTES OF JOINT CONSULTATIVE COMMITTEE MEETING</u>
> <u>HELD ON</u>
> <u>MONDAY, 15th OCTOBER 2018 AT 2.30 pm.</u>

> **EXAMPLE**
>
> RESIDENTS' ASSOCIATION: PRIORY COURT
>
> Minutes of a meeting of the
> Residents' Association of
> Priory Court
> held on 17th October 2018 at 6.30 pm
> in the Connaught Suite, Forrester's Arms, London SW1 8AB

Listing the attendees

It is important to record attendance details accurately. This basically involves the compilation of two lists: those who were 'present' and those who were 'in attendance'. The *present* list relates to members of the group who are authorised to take part in the decision-making processes and who have the power to vote. The *in attendance* list relates to people who are not members of the group, but who attended the meeting. This is an important distinction. Under common law, a quorum must exist for each item of business and a quorum can only be formed from those entitled to vote. Take, for example, a board meeting. Articles often restrict the right to vote where a director has a *personal* interest in the business being discussed. In such cases, it may be that the meeting becomes inquorate for some items. It is important, therefore, that a disinterested quorum is present for each item of business and that the minutes give enough detail to indicate this. Also, someone may attend for part of the meeting only. If, for example, a director leaves halfway through the meeting this can be recorded by making a note against the name (e.g. 'for minutes 4 to 7 only'). If a member is not present for the entire meeting (either joining late or leaving early), this can also be recorded in the main text (e.g. 'at this point, Paul Conaldi apologised and, with the chairperson's permission, left the meeting'). Similar annotations are often required for those in attendance. Take, for example, a joint consultative committee meeting, where a representative from the human resources department is invited to join the meeting for one item (the third item) to discuss a change in recruitment policy. The note against the name would simply read: '(for item 3)'.

How should the names be listed? For the present list, you should include both forename and surname and it is usual to list the name of the chairperson first and to clearly indicate their role. This is done by adding words such as 'chair', 'chairperson', or 'in the chair' next to the name. The names of the other members should be listed, by surname, in alphabetical order. For some types of meetings you may also need to indicate the department or organisation represented.

The same approach should be applied to the 'in attendance' list and remember to include yourself in this list either as 'secretary' or 'minute-taker'. You may also choose to list separately, any observers who have been invited to attend the meeting. In committee meetings, there may be occasions when the chairperson has approved a person to act as substitute (i.e. to take the place of a particular member at the meeting). In such cases, the person can be listed as 'present' with an annotation indicating the person for whom they were substituting.

With regard to general meetings of companies, it is important to record the numbers present or represented, even if the names of the members present are not recorded (to prove that a quorum existed for each item of business). The names of the directors who are present should be recorded (as 'in attendance' if they are not also members).

Some examples of attendance lists (integrated with the heading) are shown below:

> **EXAMPLE**
>
> TMF TRAINING LIMITED
>
> Minutes of a meeting of the Board
> held on 18 September 2018 commencing at 10.30 am
> in the King's Suite, 47 Rathbone Court, London NW1 7JB
>
> | Present: | Tony Stoneman | (in the chair) |
> |---|---|---|
> | | Kirsty Fuller | |
> | | Robert Lewis | (for minutes 1 to 4 only) |
> | | Alex Rachev | |
> | | James Songue | |
> | | Abbie Redgrave | |
> | | Charles Street | |
> | | Glenn Brady | |
> | In attendance: | Victoria Stair | (Company Secretary) |

> **EXAMPLE**
>
> ZAROTEC SOLUTIONS LIMITED
>
> MINUTES of the 10th ANNUAL GENERAL MEETING
> Held on Thursday, 25th October 2018 at
> Royal Hotel, 56 Long Lane, London NW2 5JG at 10.30 am.
>
> | Present: | Andrew Forde (in the chair) |
> |---|---|
> | | Dean Gates |
> | | Paul Herrera |
> | | Lyn Champion |
> | | Ruth Manu |
> | | 15 shareholders |
> | In attendance: | Jacquie Gold (Secretary) |
> | | Jeff Williams (Auditor) |

> ## EXAMPLE
>
> MINUTES OF JOINT CONSULTATIVE COMMITTEE MEETING
> HELD ON
> MONDAY, 15th OCTOBER 2018 AT 2.30 pm.
>
> Present:
> Tony Bush (Chairperson)
> Jim Bancroft (Director of Administration)
> Joe Cheeseman (Computer Services)
> Nola Davy (Middle Management)
> Bianca Evans (Purchasing)
> Shanaz Grech (Marketing)
> Pat Healy (Senior Management Team)
> Dave Merrill (IT Support)
> Tony Rhodes (Senior Management Team)
> Tony Sotinwa (Operations)
> Lana Sulca (Middle Management)
> Karen Storey (Head of Human Resources)
> Ellie Vann (Finance)
>
> In attendance:
> Anne-Marie Clarke (Minute-taker)
> Lianne Xie (Human Resources) (for item 4)
> Gary Marchant (Human Resources) (for item 4)

Apologies for absence

If people have been invited but cannot attend and send their apologies then this should be recorded. Apologies for absence, usually constitutes the first item on the agenda, but some organisations choose to list the apologies alongside the other attendance information. As the minute-taker, you may receive apologies at various points in the meeting cycle; some people may inform you at the end of the previous meeting that they will be unable to attend. Others will send apologies at some point between the two meetings and some may ask a fellow member to pass on a message at the meeting itself. Of course not all non-attendees send apologies – some people simply fail to show up! These people should not be recorded under apologies for absence. However, some organisations have created a separate list on the minutes to record these names, using the heading: 'Absent'. In theory at least, this approach enables a complete record to be maintained and flags up possible trends in non-attendance for the chairperson to address. On the other hand, it can be viewed by some as an authoritarian practice which 'advertises' the fact of non-attendance. As the minute-taker, you will obviously need to follow the agreed practice in this regard. Three examples of layout are provided opposite. The first two examples show two styles of recording apologies on the front page listing; the other example shows the recording of an apology as the first item on the agenda. It is worth remembering that apologies should normally just be recorded for group members, not for people who would normally be in attendance.

STRUCTURE, STYLE AND LAYOUT **107**

> **EXAMPLE**
>
> TMF TRAINING LIMITED
>
> Minutes of a meeting of the Board
> held on 18 September 2018 commencing at 10.30 am
> in the King's Suite, 47 Rathbone Court, London NW1 7JB
>
> | Present: | Tony Stoneman | (in the chair) |
> | --- | --- | --- |
> | | Kirsty Fuller | |
> | | Robert Lewis | (for minutes 1 to 4 only) |
> | | Alex Rachev | |
> | | James Songue | |
> | | Abbie Redgrave | |
> | | Charles Street | |
>
> | In attendance: | Victoria Stair | (Company Secretary) |
> | --- | --- | --- |
>
> An apology for absence due to illness was received from Glenn Brady and accepted

> **EXAMPLE**
>
> TMF TRAINING LIMITED
>
> Minutes of a meeting of the Board
> held on 18 September 2018 commencing at 10.30 am
> in the King's Suite, 47 Rathbone Court, London NW1 7JB
>
> | Present: | Tony Stoneman | (in the chair) | Apologies: | Glenn Brady |
> | --- | --- | --- | --- | --- |
> | | Kirsty Fuller | | | |
> | | Robert Lewis | (for minutes 1 to 4 only) | Absent: | Charles Street |
> | | Alex Rachev | | | |
> | | James Songue | | | |
> | | Abbie Redgrave | | | |
>
> | In attendance: | Victoria Stair | (Company Secretary) |
> | --- | --- | --- |

> **EXAMPLE**
>
> **1. APOLOGIES FOR ABSENCE**
>
> An apology for absence was received from Glenn Brady.

Declarations of Interest

Some organisations include Declarations of Interest as an agenda item in their meetings. With regard to conflicts of interest, the following points from ICSA's Guidance note *Minute taking* are worthy of note:

Some board minutes, especially transactional ones produced by external lawyers, include a statement that the members of the board have declared all conflicts of interest. Our consultation found that practice diverges sharply on this issue. It is a generalisation, but probably not an unfair one, to say that charities and public bodies tend to mention this issue at the start of the meeting, typically as a reminder to attendees; whilst companies tend to record conflicts of interest only when one is specifically raised at a board meeting by a board member, in which case it is noted under the relevant agenda item, when the conflicts register is circulated or tabled, or where it is necessary to note a change to the register. This may be at least partly because many companies and some public bodies have a procedure for considering, approving and recording conflicts of interest which are recorded in a register maintained by the company secretary.

It is up to each individual organisation to decide how to deal with conflicts of interest at board meetings and how these should be minuted.

For companies, sections 177 and 182 of the Act require directors to disclose their interests and so, usually, do the company's articles of association. These requirements, and any other relevant regulatory requirements relating to conflicts should always be complied with.

> **ICSA GOOD PRACTICE**
>
> **Minuting conflicts of interest**
>
> Some transactions involving the company and a director might give rise to a conflict between the interests of the company and the personal or other interests or duties of the director. An example is where the company is agreeing a director's service contract. The director has a duty to the company to get the best contractual terms for the company but this conflicts with his or her personal interest in obtaining favourable terms.
>
> Conflict of interest rules apply to protect the organisation but, generally, the director should declare any interest before the matter is discussed. Depending on the circumstances, and taking into account the relevant provisions in the organisation's constitution and applicable

ICSA GOOD PRACTICE continued

regulatory requirements, a director may be required, or may choose, to recuse themselves from discussion and decisions on these matters.

In any conflicts of interest situation it is important that the minutes note, if applicable, that the director in question was not present for, or did not contribute to, the relevant discussion.

Organisations will need to address any conflicts of interest having in mind any specific legal, regulatory or constitutional requirements that apply in their case, as well as their own preferred practice.

Once again this is a matter for individual organisations, but it seems to us that the following arrangements will, more often than not, be appropriate:

- the director should be identified in the minutes;
- the nature of the conflict, the decision as to whether or not the director should attend the section of the meeting in which he/she is conflicted and any other action taken by the board to address the conflict should be recorded in the minutes; and
- whether or not the director concerned leaves the room, the minutes should make it clear that he/she took no part in that section of the meeting and, where applicable, could confirm that the meeting remained quorate.

Minutes of the previous meeting

The purpose of this item is to approve the minutes of the previous meeting as being a true and accurate record of the proceedings. When there are no issues, the recording is straightforward as the following examples show:

EXAMPLE

2: MINUTES OF THE PREVIOUS MEETING HELD ON 16 AUGUST 2018

The minutes of the meeting held on 16 August 2018 were agreed and signed as a true and accurate record.

EXAMPLE

2: MINUTES OF THE PREVIOUS MEETING HELD ON 16 AUGUST 2018

The minutes of the board meeting held on 16 August 2018 were taken as read, approved and signed.

> **E.G. EXAMPLE**
>
> **2: MINUTES OF THE PREVIOUS MEETING HELD ON 16 AUGUST 2018**
>
> The minutes of the meeting held on 16 August 2018, having been circulated, were taken as read and were agreed.

However, there may be a need for amendments to the minutes and these can be made before the minutes have been signed as a true and accurate record by the chairperson. Efficiency on the part of everyone can minimise the need for amendments. The minute-taker should aim to produce an accurate draft and the chairperson should be diligent in reading the draft and making any necessary corrections prior to circulation. The members should ensure that they read the minutes thoroughly and make a note of any amendments prior to attending the meeting. At the meeting itself, the chairperson should be assertive in managing this section. Discussion should relate purely to matters of accuracy. Examples of approaches to recording amendments are shown below:

> **E.G. EXAMPLE**
>
> **2: MINUTES OF THE PREVIOUS MEETING HELD ON 16 AUGUST 2018**
>
> The Board agreed the minutes of the meeting held on 16 August 2018 as a true and accurate record subject to the following amendment:
>
> Page 6, paragraph 4.2: The second sentence: 'The Director of Administration informed the meeting that all departmental training budgets would be reduced by 150% in respect of the calendar year beginning January 2019' should read: 'The Director of Administration informed the meeting that all departmental training budgets would be reduced by 15% in respect of the calendar year beginning January 2019.'
>
> OR:
>
> The meeting noted that on Page 6, paragraph 4.2: The second sentence: 'The Director of Administration informed the meeting that all departmental training budgets would be reduced by 150% in respect of the calendar year beginning January 2019' should read: 'The Director of Administration informed the meeting that all departmental training budgets would be reduced by 15% in respect of the calendar year beginning January 2019.' With this amendment, the minutes were agreed as a true and accurate record.

Amendments should not be made after the minutes have been signed by the chairperson and the filed minutes of the previous meeting should not be corrected. If this was done, the amendment (recorded in the current minutes) would appear to be correcting a point that was already correct!

Not all groups insist on the signing of the minutes by the chairperson. For some groups this may be acceptable practice. However, for more formal meetings, the minutes should be signed. It has already been noted that the minutes, signed by the chairperson of the meeting, or of the subsequent meeting, are *prima facie* evidence of the proceedings. The Charity Commission in its guidelines on law and good practice at meetings emphasises that the formal minutes (approved and signed) form the only legal record of the meeting's proceedings. As case law has illustrated with regard to companies, the minutes have power as an evidential tool. If unsigned minutes are admitted as evidence of the meeting's proceedings, they will not carry the same weight as a set of minutes signed by the chairperson. The usual procedure at board meetings is for the minutes to be signed by the chairperson immediately after they have been approved as a true and accurate record.

Matters arising

In the meeting itself, this should be a succinct progress review; a straightforward item where participants provide updates on actions taken. Unfortunately, participants often view this part of the meeting as an opportunity to raise all sorts of issues from the previous meeting and/or to give 'chapter and verse' on how they completed their actions. If the chairperson fails to take control, this 'section' of the meeting can become a meeting in its own right! Obviously, some discussion may be necessary on certain issues, but as the proactive minute-taker, do encourage the chairperson to keep tight control of this section and create the right balance between the time devoted to this part of the meeting and the time allocated to discussion of the main agenda items. Examples of layout for this section are shown below; various levels of detail are illustrated.

EXAMPLE

3: MATTERS ARISING

The meeting noted that all the actions agreed at the previous meeting had either been completed or were being progressed.

112 EFFECTIVE MINUTE TAKING

> **EXAMPLE**
>
> **3: MATTERS ARISING**
>
> **3.1 Private Health Insurance** (Minute 5.2)
>
> It was agreed that discussions should be deferred until all replies had been received.
>
> **3.2 Staff Restaurant** (Minute 7)
>
> Ellie Vann confirmed that the meeting with the caterers would now take place on 7 November.
>
> **3.3 Operating Plan and Budget 2019** (Minute 8.2)
>
> Jim Bancroft informed the meeting that the one-page statement of goals for 2019 had now been approved.

Sometimes there may be a requirement for a more detailed summary. The box below shows an example of this for point 3.1 above:

> **EXAMPLE**
>
> **3.1 Private Health Insurance** (Minute 5.2)
>
> Karen Storey informed the meeting that only one reply had thus far been received out of the five health scheme operators she had written to. It was agreed that further discussions on the matter should be deferred until replies had been received from all the scheme operators consulted.

The main agenda items

These items form the 'core' of the meeting. In the previous chapter, some points were discussed regarding writing style and useful words, terms and phrases for writing up the minutes. However, when you begin to write, there are some important questions to ask yourself, such as:

- How much background detail should I include?
- Should I use people's names?
- How should I record decisions?
- How should I record actions?

The answers to these questions of course depend on the type of meeting you are minuting and the expectations of the group in terms of detail and presentation. If you have been minuting a meeting for some time, then you will not have a problem here because you will be used to managing expectations and be familiar with all the layout and style requirements. However, when you are minuting a meeting for the first time, you will need to think about these areas more carefully.

One of the guiding principles for writing the minutes for any meeting is the need to be concise (refer back to the 'eight Cs' of the minute-taking mix in Chapter 1). However, requirements regarding the level of detail will vary. You may need to write quite succinct minutes for a board meeting, but a far more detailed set for a joint consultative committee. The danger when writing longer minutes is to fall into the trap of writing *too* much. Even where a relatively detailed set of minutes is required, they should still be concise.

Should you use people's names? Some minutes omit the use of names almost entirely, but there is no reason why names cannot be used, provided a sense of balance is maintained. For example, expressions such as: 'Tony Bush reported on…', or 'Kirsty Fuller undertook to…' are fine. However, what needs to be avoided is the continual attribution of comments to individuals. It was pointed out in a previous chapter that when you are taking the notes, you are writing down points in the order they were made; you have no direct control on the way the discussion develops, which at times may be quite disjointed. However, when you are writing the minutes, you are concentrating on the logical grouping of content. This requires you to group parts of the discussion together and summarise. If you keep attributing comments to individuals, you inevitably end up tracking the process of the meeting, rather than capturing the essence of the discussion. The result makes for a long, disjointed and rather 'painful' read! So, aim to summarise parts of the discussion using phrases such as: 'following a detailed discussion', 'a discussion took place', 'overall, the members were positive', 'the board recognised that this was an urgent issue'.

How then should you record decisions and actions? Decisions are at the 'heart' of the meeting; they are what it is really all about. So, in the minutes, the decisions – and any actions resulting from them – need to stand out. Chapter 8 emphasised the importance of listening for the decisions and, of course, being a proactive minute-taker, you will have no doubt interrupted to seek clarification where necessary! So, the challenge now is not related to identifying the decisions and actions; now it is *how* to record them. Many different styles are adopted across different organisations and you will need to consider the rules, procedures and conventions within your organisation. You may also have some flexibility to design your own approach. Various examples are shown below and may stimulate some ideas!

EXAMPLE

A resolution at a general meeting

DIRECTORS' REPORT for the year ended 30 September 2019

The chairperson referred members to the Report and Accounts for the year ended 30 September 2019 and the Balance Sheet as at that date. He requested Karen Sheppard of ABC Accountants to read the audit report which she did.

EXAMPLE continued

The chairperson proposed, Richard Lees seconded and it was resolved unanimously that the report and accounts of the company for the year ended 30 September 2019 and the Balance Sheet as at that date be and they are hereby received and adopted

Adapted from 'One Stop Meetings', David Martin.

Discussion, decision and action

7: Acting Head of Department: Accounting and Finance

Detailed discussion took place regarding whether the appointment should be advertised to senior staff in other departments or restricted to senior staff currently working in the Accounting and Finance Department.

Decision: It was agreed that the appointment should be made from senior staff currently working in Accounting and Finance and that the Director of Administration would speak initially to the four staff concerned in order to gauge the level of interest.

Action: The Director of Administration to meet with all four staff within the next two weeks and report back at the next meeting.

EXAMPLE

Short statement of agreement and action

Following discussion, It was **agreed** that the Marketing Department would discuss the proposal in greater depth outside the meeting and report back at the next meeting.

Action: Shanaz Grech

EXAMPLE

More than one action

9: Senior Management Team: 'Away day'

Jon Mayor reminded the meeting of the need to finalise the arrangements for the forthcoming senior management team planning 'away day' on 13 November. Following discussion, It was **agreed** that the Regency Hotel should be booked for the event and the booking should include the hire of the large meeting room (including audio-visual facilities) and lunch for 12 people.

> **EXAMPLE continued**
>
> **Action:**
>
> | | |
> |---|---|
> | Conference facilities to be booked with update at next meeting | Lin Yan |
> | Lunch arrangements to be finalised and booked with update at next meeting | Chris Clark |

> **EXAMPLE**
>
> **Introductory comment framing the wording of a resolution**
>
> Jon Mayor expressed concern over the current situation and proposed to the meeting the following **resolution**, which was subsequently **passed unanimously**:
>
> [TEXT OF THE RESOLUTION]

Of course decisions are not always reached and action is not always required. The important thing is to ensure that the reader is not 'left hanging'; the discussion should always be 'rounded-out' nicely so that people are not left asking questions.

Some meetings include a section just prior to the main agenda items headed 'correspondence', 'reports' or 'information only'. These are not discussion items; the purpose is to receive the paper, not discuss it. Ideally, reports should be circulated with the agenda. In such cases there is no need to minute what is said; you can simply draw attention to the report, for example: 'The meeting noted the report on graduate recruitment trends.' That said, practice at meetings in this connection varies; sometimes you may be expected to provide a short summary in the minutes and, if the report is purely verbal, then you would need to provide a short summary or obtain a copy and attach it to the minutes.

Sometimes the discussion results in a 'referral' or a 'deferral'. A referral is where the item is passed to another group, so instead of the action point, the minutes could simply say, for example: 'Referred to the International Relations Committee for further guidance'. A deferral is where a decision has been made to discuss the item at a future meeting, for example: 'Due to the delay in receiving the quotations, it was agreed that further discussions on the proposal would be deferred to the next meeting'.

ICSA GOOD PRACTICE

Level of detail in minutes

ICSA's views on the relevant considerations are:

- **Minutes should not be a verbatim record.** They should summarise the key points of discussion but focus on the decision or, in the case of a committee meeting, any recommendation to the board.
- **Minutes should document the reasons for the decision and include sufficient background information for future reference** – or, perhaps, for someone not at the meeting to understand why the board has taken the decision that it has. In simple terms, their purpose is to record what was done, not what was said but with sufficient context to give assurance that it was done properly.
- **If board papers are received for noting and no decision is required,** then unless there is material discussion that needs to be recorded, minutes should indicate that the relevant report was 'received (or reviewed, if that is what happened) and its contents noted'.
- **Minutes should include allocated actions.** We recommend that inclusion of actions is important, especially for committees, as they provide evidence of discharging duties and effectively challenging management, ensure accountability and that agreed actions are not overlooked.
- **Board papers should be retained, but not necessarily retained with the minutes.** On balance it seems sensible to us that all papers be retained with, although not normally as part of, the minutes of the meeting, but this is a matter for individual organisations to decide.
- **Writing minutes for regulatory oversight.** Minutes should reflect the business and sector of the organisation. Larger, more complex companies and those in regulated industries have additional issues to consider and tend to have longer meetings, so the minutes should reflect this. Minutes of board meetings in some sectors such as financial services have become more detailed and prescriptive in recent years due to increased regulatory oversight and the need to demonstrate appropriate participation and challenge by individual directors.

ICSA GOOD PRACTICE

Naming names

In our research, it became clear that practice is changing in this area, particularly in the corporate sector. A number of respondents to our consultation and attendees at our roundtables reported that there can be circumstances in which they find it necessary to record individual names so as to demonstrate individual director participation and challenge, particularly where the performance of the director might be scrutinised by the regulator.

Equally it became clear that the charity and public sectors have very different practice – and always have had – whereby individual contributions are often attributed. In some cases this reflects a regulatory or constitutional requirement, but how and where the minutes are to be made available is also an important consideration.

> ### ICSA GOOD PRACTICE continued
>
> It will normally be appropriate to name individuals who:
>
> - present a paper or report to the board;
> - are charged with specific actions or to whom responsibility has been delegated by the board;
> - have declared a potential or actual conflict of interest or similar;
> - abstain from a vote or recuse themselves;
> - request that their name be noted as dissenting from a particular decision;
> - make a recommendation, provide information or answer a question based on their special expertise on the subject, for example the Chief Executive or Finance Director;
> - are the subject of personnel issues under discussion such as appointments, reappointments or resignations; or of discussions on board effectiveness.
>
> It may, depending on the circumstances, also be appropriate to name individuals who:
>
> - request that their name be noted in a particular minute;
> - object to or dissent from a decision;
> - ask a specific question; and
> - make a particularly important or significant comment.

Any other business

This item was discussed in detail in Chapter 6. For the purpose of the minutes, it is treated in the same way as the other main agenda items and is numbered in the same way; so the main heading: 'Any other business' follows on numerically from the previous agenda item with numbered sub-headings for each of the topics.

Date of next meeting

Record here the date, time and place for the next meeting. You could also draw attention to the final date for receipt of agenda items for the next meeting and the relevant contact details. The last task is to note the time the meeting closed; for example: 'There being no further business, the meeting closed at 4.30 p.m.'

Numbering of the minutes

There are various systems for numbering your minutes, so it is worth checking what the practice is in your organisation. If you have some freedom to decide on the approach then try not to over-complicate the issue!

Many organisations start each set of minutes at '1'and follow on numerically throughout the set. Sub-headings can be given their own number e.g. 4.1, 4.2, 4.3 etc. Another approach is to number the minutes consecutively throughout the calendar year. For example: '01/2019' would be the first minute of the first meeting in 2019. As the year progressed, the number represented by the first two digits would increase sequentially; so, later on in the year, the minute number might show, for example: '92/2019'. Another variation is to include the month and abbreviate the year. So for a meeting held in April (where the first minute for this meeting is number 64 for the year), the numbering might appear like this: '64/04/19'.

Another variation is to include the nature of the meeting by means of initials. For example, the seventh minute in the calendar year 2019 of a Management Committee meeting would be: 'MC/19/007'.

The guiding principles for accurate minute writing (see again the 'eight Cs' of the minute-taking mix in Chapter 1) apply just as much to the numbering system as the composition of the main text. So, whatever system you choose, aim to be consistent.

Proofreading the minutes

When you've finally completed the writing of the minutes, there's an important stage to go through before you think about circulation: you must prof read your wok ... oh, many apologies: that should have read: you must proofread your work!

This is probably the last thing you want to do after all the concentration and effort that has gone into the writing phase, but it is essential; you want to present work which looks professional and which adds to your credibility. When proofreading, you need to be objective, so it as a good idea to leave a gap between the conclusion of writing and the commencement of proofreading; your mind will be too 'fuzzy' immediately following the writing phase.

When proofreading, you need to refer to the minute-taking mix table from Chapter 1. This will remind you of the guiding principles for accurate minute-writing as you start the checking process. The table is reproduced below.

Table 10.1: The minute-taking mix

Guiding principle	Key points
Concise	Short and succinct; emphasis on decisions
Complete	All key elements of the meeting recorded
Consistent	Uniform approach to structure and style
Clear	Unambiguous; accessible; readable
Compliant	Observing set standards and conventions
Clean	Objective and 'clutter-free'
Correct	Accurate information; accurate writing
Coherent	Logical development of material

With regard to the points in the table, ask yourself the following questions:

- Is the overall presentation and layout pleasing to the eye?
- Has objectivity been maintained throughout?
- Are all paragraphs and sentences of the correct length?
- Has consistency been maintained in the amount of background and discussion detail provided in the main agenda items?
- Is there evidence of effective summarising?
- Have too many comments been attributed to individuals?
- Do the decisions and action points clearly stand out?
- Has the material been developed in a logical way?
- Have some words been repeated too often?
- Is the vocabulary varied enough?
- Are there any unnecessary repetitions of the same point?
- Is all the necessary information included in the heading?
- Are there any errors in grammar, spelling and punctuation?
- Are the minutes factually correct throughout?
- Has use of the past tense been consistently applied?
- Are there any errors in the numbering system?

Circulating the minutes

You are now in a position to send the draft minutes to the chairperson for approval. You are working to your meeting cycle timeline, so it is important that the chairperson is encouraged to acknowledge this and return the amended draft promptly. You then need to make the final corrections to the draft minutes prior to circulation. If you are working with a new chairperson you may find that more amendments are made than you believe to be necessary. As the relationship develops, expectations on both sides will become clearer and a professional understanding will likely develop so, be patient and proactively manage the relationship!

When circulating the minutes, you must work from an accurate distribution list. If any papers were distributed at the meeting, then ensure that you attach these to the minutes for the benefit of the non-attendees. The distribution list should be kept in your strategy file for each meeting and updated when necessary.

ICSA GOOD PRACTICE

Editing draft minutes

In our opinion, it should be for the company secretary, in discussion with the chairman, to decide to whom the draft minutes should be submitted for technical review and whether their suggestions should be adopted.

ICSA GOOD PRACTICE continued

The company secretary may pass sections of the minutes recording a technical presentation or other technical matter to the relevant executive(s) for comment before submitting the draft to the chairman for review.

If minutes are well written there may be little need for editing by the directors, but that is not to say that such editing is a bad thing, or that it should be discouraged. It is, of course, absolutely right that the board and others in attendance provide input to the editing process once the company secretary has provided a draft and rewording may help with clarity. The central issue is to ensure that the organisation's permanent record of the meeting is as correct, and as useful, as it may be.

Filing the minutes

Check the procedures for filing the minutes relating to your organisation and discuss the procedures with the chairperson concerned. Requirements will vary depending on the nature of the meeting, but you need to be clear about what is to be filed (e.g. the minutes, agenda and background papers). For companies, there are statutory requirements regarding the form in which minutes should be kept and retention of minutes, so ensure that you are clear on what is expected of you as the minute-taker regarding filing tasks.

ICSA GOOD PRACTICE

Retention of board minutes

The Act requires that corporate board minutes be retained for at least ten years. Our experience is that in many cases they are retained for much longer – and our recommendation has always been that they be retained for the life of the organisation. This may be required in any event, in particular for minutes prepared before the Act came into force as there was no time limit under the Companies Act 1985. The organisation's constitution may also include a provision about the retention of documents. The minutes should obviously be stored securely, and a pdf copy of the signed hard copy of the minutes can be used to act as a back-up (for each other).

Summary

This chapter has focused in detail on the structure of the final minutes and the information which needs to be included in each section. It has also addressed some of the tasks you will need to complete following the writing of the minutes. You will necessarily need to adapt the examples to your own particular requirements and these will inevitably vary to *some* extent depending on the nature of the meeting and the specific conventions procedures and expectations unique to your organisation.

The information presented in this chapter and the previous two chapters has related directly to the 'core' of the minute-taking function (i.e. the taking of the notes and the writing of the final minutes). The final four chapters address a variety of topics associated with the minute-taking process, beginning with the use of technology.

11
Technology and the minute-taking process

The technological revolution has affected just about everyone on this planet and the pace of change over the past few decades has been breathtaking. Businesses and households have access to a range of computer technology devices and communication and social interaction has been revolutionised with the introduction of e-mail, instant messaging, smartphones and the use of social media. At the heart of the revolution is the internet, which has brought a world of information to the fingertips of millions. Think about this book that you are reading: how would all the researching, writing, editing and publishing activities have been carried out without the use of technology?

So, technology is here to stay. Everyone has to continually make choices regarding the application of technology in their personal and professional lives and that includes you as a minute-taker! The purpose of this chapter is to consider some of the technological tools and devices which may impact on the minute-taking process. The aim is not simply to describe the tools, but rather to highlight the advantages and disadvantages of different approaches. As a minute-taker, you need to make informed choices regarding the use of technology in the context of your own role. The simple principle is this: The application of technology must contribute in some way to the effectiveness of the minute-taking process.

Note the term used in the chapter heading: 'minute-taking process'. It is important to recognise that technology can be applied to many of the activities you will undertake throughout the process (i.e. before, during and after the meeting).

STOP AND THINK

Think about all the different activities that you undertake as part of the minute-taking process and consider the following:

(a) What activities involve the use of technology?
(b) What are the activities in which you find technology to be particularly useful? Why is this?
(c) Are there any activities for which you deem the use of technology to be inappropriate? If so, why do you feel this way?

You will have probably have identified many areas where you incorporate the use of technology at various points during the minute-taking process. Question (c) above is an interesting one because some people are strong advocates for the increased adoption of technology in minute-taking activities. Where do you stand on the issue? The following section examines the application of several technological tools and highlights their potential advantages and disadvantages.

The laptop

The use of personal computers in the minute-taking process is well-established and it would be almost impossible to undertake the process effectively without word processing power! However, what about using a laptop to take notes during the meeting? The following table outlines the possible advantages and disadvantages.

Table 11.1 Laptops: Advantages and disadvantages

Advantages	Disadvantages
Some people find it easier to type rather than to write using a pen	Unless you are using a quiet keyboard the noise generated can be a distraction and/or irritation to participants
Templates can be easily created and stored in the computer ready for use	Some note-takers find it harder to concentrate using a laptop so prefer to use pen and paper
It may be easier to write up the final minutes if you have the established template and all your notes from the meeting in front of you	Because of the increased speed when typing there can be a tendency to write too much
Most minute-takers are proficient at word processing so it is usually quicker to type than write with a pen	There can be a tendency to fall into the trap of following the discussion and typing in parallel with the speaker rather than listening first and then noting the key points. This can affect the style of the minutes; they can become a list of who said what, rather than a summary of the decisions and the reasons for them
Legibility should be improved. Although typing errors may creep in due to tiredness, they are more easily identifiable	If too much is written, any time saved by use of the laptop may be negated by a longer process of grouping and summarising later on
A range of word processing features are readily available to use	Computers can malfunction at the most inappropriate times
It is arguably easier and more time-efficient to make any corrections to the notes using a computer rather than by hand	The use of a laptop can be distracting for others. Eyes seem to veer naturally towards the note-taker

Table 11.1 *continued*

Advantages	Disadvantages
In theory, it will be possible for the final minutes to be produced within a shorter timeframe than would otherwise be the case	It can be awkward having to scroll through the text if certain sections need to be re-visited
You have your personal reference files stored on the laptop which can provide a valuable reference source should it be required in the meeting	The use of certain note-taking techniques (e.g. spider diagrams and visual recording) may pose practical challenges
If internet facilities are available you also have access to all the information on the world wide web. There may be situations where this research facility can contribute to resolving any issues or knowledge gaps on the part of the participants	If you are too focused on your screen, you may fail to get the real sense of the discussion. Looking at the speaker and reading body language can be helpful, but there may be a tendency to ignore this if you are too absorbed with typing

Clearly there are a number of factors which need to be weighed up on both sides when you are deciding whether to use a laptop to take notes. If you decide that the advantages outweigh the disadvantages, then make sure you remember the following:

- Use a quiet keyboard in order to avoid distractions.
- Avoid writing too much.
- Periodically look up and make eye contact with the speaker just as you would if you were taking notes using a pen.
- Ensure that your focus on the screen doesn't prevent you from making necessary interventions (e.g. interrupting to ask for clarification and communicating with the chairperson).
- Save your work frequently.
- Take a pen and paper as a back-up.
- After the meeting, print-off a hard copy of the notes as an 'insurance policy'.
- Be aware of confidentiality. Your laptop will contain many files perhaps of a confidential nature, so look after your machine!
- A laptop is a substitute for a paper notebook; that is the only difference. Everything else about your approach should be the same. The 'LEARN' technique needs to be applied irrespective of whether you use pen or a computer.

Writing the minutes in the meeting

There may be some meetings where the minutes can be written up during the meeting itself. This is controversial, because the very idea appears to undermine the requirement for considered thought prior to grouping and summarising elements of the discussion and then presenting the final minutes in the logical order of content rather than in the order of the discussion. This is true; however, there may be some meetings which, by their nature, lend themselves to this type of approach. It is usual practice in such meetings for no notes to be taken during the actual discussion. However, the chairperson summarises the decisions at the end of each item of discussion, the minute-taker then composes the minute which is subsequently read out to secure agreement. In such cases, the use of a laptop may be an advantage. Templates can be prepared in advance containing many of the necessary headings and details. The information added during the meeting can then be inserted quite easily.

It might also be acceptable to use a laptop to produce a final set of notes during the meeting itself for some *informal* meetings (e.g. a team briefing where a summary of key action points is required). It is also worth noting that there are some meetings that require almost verbatim notes, for example, disciplinary hearings. These are really meeting notes rather than minutes, but if you are a very good typist using a laptop can work well here – as can recording.

Recording devices

Some people like the idea of using a recording device because they believe it resolves the question 'What happens if I miss something?' However, in practice, it creates more problems than solutions. Here are some of the potential disadvantages:

CHECKLIST

- Participants may feel apprehensive or uneasy about being recorded.
- Background noise may dilute the quality of the recording.
- Depending on the equipment used, there may be a need to replenish power or move to another device in order to continue. This will be distracting for everyone.
- There are no visual clues to help the minute-taker identify who is speaking.
- It can be hard to make out exactly what people are saying, particularly if the 'quality' of the contribution is poor (e.g. mumbling, waffling, talking over other people, lowering volume at the end of sentences etc).
- There is always the risk that the equipment will malfunction.
- The minute-taker can become distracted worrying about how well the device is working.
- If recordings are made to provide evidence of the proceedings of the meeting, in case anyone falsifies the minutes, then there is a need to address this as an organisational issue.
- If recordings are made to provide proof in case the accuracy of the minutes is questioned, then again this is an organisational issue which needs to be addressed; the minute-taker is part of a team. Everyone should respect the agreed conventions and procedures for ensuring accuracy.
- If recordings are made so that the minute-taker can go back and check the accuracy of what was said (when writing up the minutes), then this creates an onerous task, The minute-taker will have to 'trawl' through the recording trying to locate the required information.
- If recordings are made to constitute the main form of 'minute-taking' then this is a pointless exercise. The minute-taker has to go through the whole recording after the event to pick out the key points; the better solution is simply to take effective notes at the meeting.
- There are legal requirements to getting participants' agreement to a recording.

The use of recording devices is probably not a sensible idea if employed as a regular feature to 'aid' minute-taking for the reasons described above. However, the practice may arguably have some value as a back-up in certain one-off situations (e.g. in recording workshops or group sessions where a significant amount of discussion is involved).

> **ICSA GOOD PRACTICE**
>
> **Retention of recordings**
>
> Some company secretaries have adopted the practice of audio recording board meetings.
> We would suggest that the retention period for these recordings will be a function of the purpose of the recording. Where it is an aide-memoire for the company secretary then it would seem sensible for it to be destroyed once the minutes have been approved; if the primary purpose of recording is transparency, for example where audio-visual recording or live streaming is used, typically in the public sector, they may be retained for a longer period or permanently.

The use of smartpens

One technological innovation, which may capture the imagination of some minute-takers, is the smartpen. This is a tool which actually records the words that people are speaking, but also links them to the notes that the pen holder is taking. So, if you really wanted to, you could record the entire meeting and then replay any part of that meeting simply by tapping the tip of the pen at the appropriate point on the notes page! For example, if say, you took 15 pages of notes at the meeting, and you found a point needing clarification on page 9, you would tap the pen on the relevant point and the pen would then play back exactly what you heard at the time you wrote down that point. Smartpens are very 'high-tech' devices and require some initial configuration. However, after this has been completed, the user simply writes with the device as if it were a 'normal' pen. Obviously, this device will not work on ordinary paper; special interactive notepaper is required which can be obtained from smartpen retailers.

Advocates would argue that the smartpen gives you the 'best of both worlds'. You still take your notes in the usual way, but you have the added back up of the recording if you really get stuck.

There may be some potential ethical issues to consider with the use of smartpens. For example, some participants feel uneasy about being recorded, so, if you are recording the entire meeting and nobody in the room knows about it you could be challenged on this if someone found out. A clear explanation of what you are doing and why at the outset may obviate this potential concern. Also, smartpens are not particularly cheap, so you would need to evaluate the potential benefits (ask for a demonstration or ask a colleague who is a user) before making the investment.

Whenever you use a technological device for the first time, you may discover that the practice doesn't live up to the promise. So, you need to make sure that if you use a smartpen, it really does work for *you*.

The impact of technology on the management of meetings

As a proactive minute-taker, it also a good idea to think about the impact technology has made, and can make, on the management of meetings. This will impact on your role as a note-taker and will also be relevant if part of your role involves the selection and booking of IT facilities and equipment for meetings.

Virtual meetings

A virtual meeting is one where the participants are not gathered together physically in the same place, but can use videoconferencing or teleconferencing facilities to engage in discussions and make decisions. In today's fast-paced business environment, virtual meetings have a number of advantages as follows:

- Significant cost savings can be achieved:
  - Travel costs
  - Accommodation and subsistence costs.
- Less time is wasted in travelling, thus it can be efficiently utilised on other activities.
- Virtual meetings create a greater element of flexibility.
- There is less disruption to schedules; planning is easier.

However, there are some disadvantages:

- They can be difficult to manage effectively if the group is too large.
- The technology needs to be used effectively.
- Preparation needs to be very thorough.
- Greater consideration needs to be given to choice of words and expressions, in order to convey the correct meaning.
- Effective listening techniques need to be employed.
- For videoconferencing, clear visibility needs to be maintained.
- For teleconferencing, a sense of order must be maintained.
- Respect for all participants should be evident throughout.
- Business should always be transacted in a professional manner.

How do virtual meetings impact on you as a minute-taker? First, the meeting needs to be chaired effectively, so it is good to work as closely as possible with the chairperson in connection with all arrangements for the meeting. There should be an understanding that the chairperson will provide regular summaries of the key points. Second, the participants are likely to 'flag' more easily in a virtual meeting due to the demands which are inherent in this form of meeting. This may impact the quality of contributions, so be extra vigilant in terms of your own focused concentration. Also, encourage the chair to effectively time manage. An overly long meeting of this nature will be unproductive. Finally, discipline yourself mentally to concentrate on the meeting at hand and not the inevitable distractions that will occur from time to time.

Meeting administration

Technology can assist you greatly in connection with many of the activities that you need to undertake before, during and after the meeting. The following checklist provides one or two simple reminders and suggestions:

> **CHECKLIST**
>
> - As the proactive minute-taker, make sure that you are thoroughly familiar with all the technological options available for use in connection with meetings. You may need to advise the chairperson on the benefits and limitations of different approaches and the likely impact on the effectiveness of the meeting.
> - Ensure that you always maintain a 'clean' filing system on your own computer. Always aim to be well organised and know exactly where to locate the information you need.
> - With regard to the advice given in Chapter 5 (i.e. the need to create a strategy file for each of the meetings you minute) make sure that this file is as comprehensive as possible for each meeting. Include all your checklists, reference notes, templates etc. and make sure the files are regularly updated.
> - Think how you can make greater use of technology to be proactive in your minute-taking activities. For example, using e-mail to give reminders of deadlines in connection with the meeting cycle, or sending reference material to participants electronically.

Electronic archiving

Regarding minutes, technology can be utilised in developing electronic archiving systems. If you are involved in the filing of minutes then it is good to encourage your organisation to assess the effectiveness of current systems and consider the possibility of change if needed. It is not the purpose of this section to discuss electronic archiving processes in detail; simply to provide a few reminders and suggestions regarding the development of electronic systems: Please note the following:

- If you are thinking about electronic archiving, thorough and detailed planning is necessary.
- Study examples of electronic systems in other organisations and become conversant with the advantages and possible drawbacks.
- Design the system to be user-friendly.
- Plan the search facility very carefully to ensure that it meets user needs.
- Treat the introduction of electronic archiving as a project and plan accordingly.
- Consult appropriate experts when planning the system.
- Ensure that back-up systems are put in place.

Summary

This chapter has examined the use of several technological tools in connection with the minute-taking process, namely, laptops, recording devices and smartpens. It has also addressed some of the salient issues for minute-takers with regard to virtual meetings. Technology is advancing every day and new tools and devices seem to hit the market with increasing frequency. However, whatever the nature of the device you might be thinking about using, there is a key principle to keep in mind: *The use of technology should always enhance the effectiveness of the minute-taking process, never detract from it*.

The three chapters which follow are concerned with looking at the interpersonal skills and personal qualities that are important for proactive minute takers. The importance of communication skills and effective listening, are highlighted in Chapter 12.

12
Communication skills and the minute-taker

Olleh, eht srohtua fo siht koob era gnilliw ot evig uoy ytfif dnasuoht sdnuop, on snoitseuq deksa; lla uoy evah ot od si tcatnoc lihP sivaD yb liame nihtiw eht txen ytxis sdnoces.

Did you understand that message? If you did you're a genius! Unfortunately for you, the message is written backwards. What it actually says is:

Hello, the authors of this book are willing to give you fifty thousand pounds, no questions asked; all you have to do is contact Phil Davis by e-mail within the next 60 seconds.

Because you didn't understand the message and were probably somewhat bemused trying to decipher it, you've missed out on a golden opportunity. If, by some amazing stroke of good fortune, you were able to understand it and happened to be sitting right next to your computer when reading it, then Phil Davis is in big trouble!

Imagine that that was a real offer and you missed out on it purely through your inability to understand the message! On a serious note though, there are occasions, which sometimes occur on a daily basis, where messages fail to be understood due to some form of communication barrier. How often do you say something like: 'sorry I didn't quite catch that', or 'would you mind repeating that'? You ask these questions because you haven't fully understood the message. The minute-taking role is characterised by *a need to understand*. Some of your understanding is acquired through reading written material, but in many situations and certainly within the meeting itself, your understanding is based on your interpretation of *interpersonal* communication. In this chapter, the importance of effective interpersonal communication is discussed in the context of the minute-taking role. This will involve first, an analysis of the '3 Vs' of interpersonal communication and second, the critical importance of active listening.

The '3Vs' of communication

With regard to interpersonal communication, impressions are created in three ways:

- Verbally   (what is said)
- Vocally   (how it's said)
- Visually   (the visual signals on display while it's being said)

You need to appreciate the importance of the '3Vs' with regard to the following:

- Understanding and evaluating the messages being communicated by others
- Considering the effectiveness of your own communication.

Verbal

This relates to *what* is actually said. When people speak, they select words and group them together to convey a message. The *choice* of words and phrases, then, is very important. You know from experience that communication can suffer if the words fail to create meaning in the mind of the receiver. For example, if you are sitting in a meeting and someone is using many technical terms which are unfamiliar to you, vital parts of their message may be lost.

Vocal

Vocal communication relates to *how* something is said (i.e. the use of the voice). Again, you know from experience that some people speak very softly whereas others speak loudly. Also, people vary in terms of the pace of their speech and the timbre of their voice; some voices sound powerful and full bodied, whereas others may sound thin and weak by comparison. In addition, some voices are very 'colourful' whereas others are monotone. At a meeting, you will probably find that a wide variety of vocal styles is in evidence!

Visual

Visual communication relates to the body language signals conveyed by the speaker and the speaker's appearance. Again, from experience, you know that some people are very animated when they speak, whereas others are a lot less expansive. Some people appear very confident when speaking, whereas others may visibly display signs of nerves. Also, the appearance of individuals varies considerably, not just in style of attire, but in attention to detail (or lack of it).

Which of the '3Vs' do you consider to be the most important? There have been many studies into this over the years but a generally accepted view is illustrated by the pie chart opposite.

The fact that just 8% is attached to the importance of verbal communication surprises some people. The '3Vs' of course, are not mutually exclusive. Interrelationships between all become apparent and conclusions will be drawn from this.

Think about this scenario: You are giving a presentation to a high-profile group of business people. You are presenting a serious message with much supporting data in the form of detailed financial analyses. Imagine that you turned up to the presentation in a clown's costume and began to speak in an extremely high-pitched and 'nasally' voice. How seriously would your audience take you? They would pay very little attention to what you were saying; they would be very distracted by the way you were saying it and they would be totally transfixed by your appearance while you were saying it!

The above scenario illustrates the need to take into consideration all three forms of communication, but to recognise that people take notice of the visual and the vocal far more than the verbal. Consider now the two areas of importance for you as a minute-taker:

COMMUNICATING FIRST IMPRESSIONS

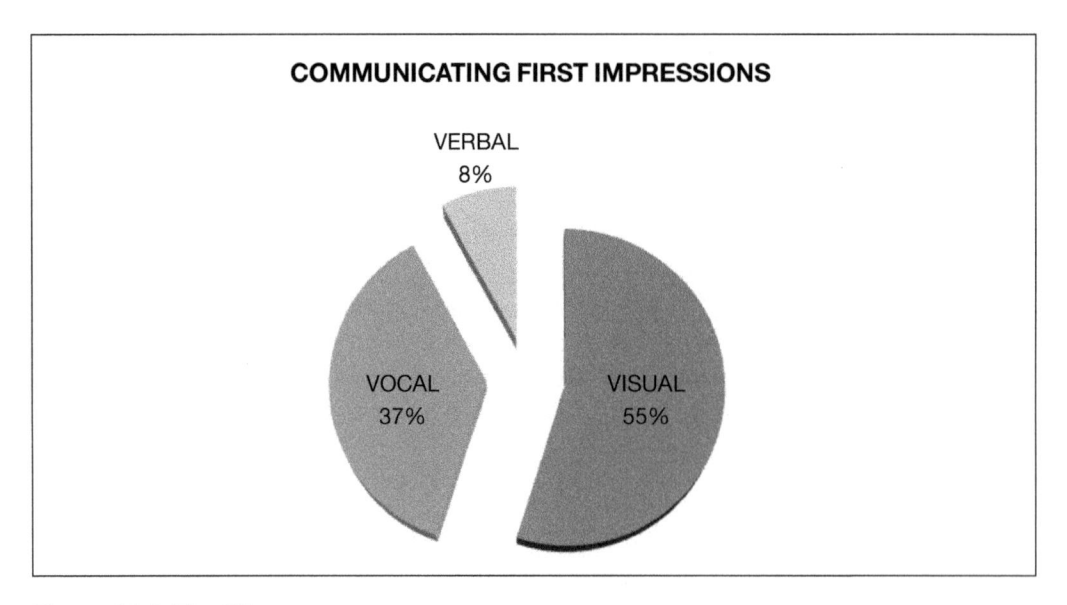

- VERBAL 8%
- VOCAL 37%
- VISUAL 55%

Figure 12.1: The 3Vs

Understanding and evaluating the messages being communicated by others

STOP AND THINK

Take a few minutes to give some thought to the following:

You are continually required to make sense of what participants are trying to communicate in a meeting. Thinking of the points discussed regarding the relative importance of the '3 Vs', how do you think your knowledge of this can help you when seeking to understand participants during the meeting and also in any interpersonal exchanges you may have outside of the meeting?

How did you get on? There are actually a number of learning points which can be drawn from a consideration of the '3Vs' which can help you to understand and evaluate the messages communicated by participants. A few ideas are listed in the checklist opposite.

> ### CHECKLIST
>
> #### A 3V checklist
>
> - Always look for changes in body language. This can signal, for example, sudden interest or the touching of a raw nerve.
> - Be aware of cultural perspectives. If there is a broad cultural mix at the meeting, remember that words mean different things to different people. Be careful with your interpretations.
> - Recognise that you will be affected by the way people express themselves, so be determined not to let voice tone or character distract you from concentrating on the main message.
> - When a verbal and a visual message conflict, people tend to believe the visual. So, take careful note of body language and the 'style' of expression used. The real meaning may be quite different from the apparent reason as described by the words. For example, if a participant says: 'Oh yeah, I agree alright' with expressive facial gestures and a sarcastic tone, then that participant probably disagrees quite strongly.
> - If you need to approach participants before or after the meeting, in order to clarify a point of concern or something you didn't quite understand, then be aware that you will be strongly influenced by visual and vocal factors. Do not to let this put you off approaching a participant if you need to clarify a point. For example, a strong voice or body language which makes you feel a little intimidated can knock you off your stride; be determined not to let it!
> - Conversely, if you are sensitive to the messages being conveyed through body language, you will know whether it is an appropriate time to approach a participant. Perhaps someone is genuinely stressed or worried about something, so judge the moment and be discerning.
> - You may miss important visual signals if you always have your head stuck in your notes! Periodically look up and make eye contact with the participants. This will be easier to do if you are applying the 'LEARN' technique.

So, there are a number of subtle areas to consider regarding the '3Vs' in connection with understanding and evaluating the messages being communicated by others. Making the effort will be worthwhile because you will find you are able to focus more on the main message; you will also pick up signals and clues as to meaning that you may otherwise have missed.

Considering the effectiveness of your own communication

As noted throughout this book, minute-takers do not play an entirely passive role. You will be required to communicate with the chairperson and also with the other meeting contributors – to a greater or lesser degree – during the course of the meeting. This communication might sometimes be extremely subtle and low key, while at other times, it may be more direct. You will also need to speak with participants outside the meeting from time to time regarding various matters. If you are proactive then you will want to be noticed by others and acknowledged as a fellow professional. You will enthusiastically approach people to assist where you need support and/or clarification on points you are unsure of.

Thinking carefully about the impression you create on other people in terms of the '3Vs' is therefore very important. For example, if you are going to interrupt in a meeting to seek clarification on a matter, then the way you use your *voice* is important. You need to be able to express yourself clearly and audibly. Therefore, you need to look at the person you are talking to and project your voice, particularly if the meeting room is large and there are a lot of people seated around the table. The problem is that you may be experiencing a degree of nervousness, particularly if you are shy or you feel a little intimidated by the group. Your vocal cords tighten when you are nervous, which results in a higher pitch than usual, so, if you end up sounding like a strangled cat, you now know why! Therefore, you need to work to control your nerves. Remember that you have the right to be there and you are interrupting because you are seeking to clarify a point for professional reasons. Also, the more proactive you are in being involved where necessary, the more confident you will feel; this will relax you and improve the quality of your voice. Also remember that the power in your voice comes, not from shouting, but from good projection. To project well, you need to breathe deeply from the diaphragm, make eye contact with the person to whom you are speaking and be free of nerves. You also need to speak at a comfortable pace. Again, nerves can serve to quicken your pace, so really work at mastering your nerves.

Visual signals are also very important. Think how you appear to others when you are communicating. For example, if you say that you are confident, but as you are saying it you are shaking like a leaf, you know which signal they will believe!

Also be conscious of your body language when conversing with people outside the meeting itself. If you feel nervous, shy or intimidated then your body language will reflect this. Try to remain calm and poised. Take a genuine interest in other people and enjoy conversing with them. This will make you less self-aware.

Think also about your appearance. Ensure that it is professional and appropriate for the occasion. Your appearance should never detract from the message you are trying to convey. The following checklist will help you to build credibility as a communicator at meetings. Some of the points relate to your possible involvement as a contributor.

CHECKLIST

How to be a credible communicator

- Employ 'voice power' when speaking, but remember, power comes from projection not just volume.
- Master your nerves before entering the meeting room; if you do not, the quality of your communication will be affected. One way of achieving this is to be thoroughly prepared. Also, it may be a good idea to rehearse (without being too rigid) what you are going to say. Obviously this does not apply to interrupting to clarify a point during the meeting itself, but there may be something you need to discuss with a participant and you can prepare beforehand.
- Always be conscious of the messages your body language is conveying and be sensitive to the non-verbal clues given out by others.

CHECKLIST continued

- Always try to tailor your message to the world of the receiver.
- Be aware of the negative peer pressure in a meeting situation. Have the confidence to express yourself and your views.
- Remember: 'First impressions are lasting impressions'. Be conscious of your appearance. Anything that detracts from the message will result in poor comprehension on the part of the listener.
- Always maintain good eye contact when speaking. 'Move around' the audience and involve everyone (contributor).
- Make use of gestures to emphasise or describe parts of your message.
- Be enthusiastic. Convey self-belief in your message (particularly when contributing).
- Be aware of cultural perspectives. If there is a broad cultural mix at the meeting, remember that words mean different things to different people. Think carefully about the words you use.
- If you decide to employ visual aids to make a point, remember that these should be aids. The main communicator and persuader must be you (contributor).
- SMILE! A smile is your greatest dress accessory. It conveys warmth and draws people in.
- Employ effective questioning techniques to check understanding. Rather than a closed question (e.g. 'Do you understand?') use open-ended ones to test understanding (e.g. 'What do you understand about…?'). This is useful for contributing and in pre- and post-meeting discussion. Remember that skilled communication is a learned art. Practice is essential, so make inter-personal skills a subject for your personal development programme (see Chapter 14).

Active listening

Naturally, listening is one of the most important skills in the toolkit of all minute-takers. However, not all people listen well. *Hearing*, of course, is not the same as *listening*. Imagine that you are standing at a bus stop. There are two people next to you having a conversation and you are reading a newspaper. You can hear the people talking (i.e. the sounds are audible) but you are not listening to what they are saying; you are not actively involved in listening to the discussion to discern the message. A minute-taker needs to listen actively to understand the main message. However, this can sometimes present a challenge.

STOP AND THINK

Take a few minutes to give some thought to the following:

There are a number of barriers to effective listening. Think about the meetings that you minute. What barriers to active listening have you encountered?
   In your opinion, what is necessary to successfully negotiate barriers to listening?

What barriers did you identify? Unfortunately, the barriers are not always factors that we can fully control, so we have to learn how to negotiate them. The following table summarises some of the common barriers to active listening.

Table 12.1: Barriers to active listening

Barriers to active listening

- Noise – literal
- Noise – figurative (distracting thoughts)
- Deep prejudice (on the part of the listener)
- Cynicism (towards what is being said)
- Poor powers of concentration
- Unstructured arguments (by participants)
- Poor communication skills displayed by contributors
- Poor chairing skills

For you as a minute-taker, it is unlikely that you will have too many problems with points 3 and 4 above. However, if you are contributing to the meeting as well, these factors could possibly come in to play. If you diligently apply the 'LEARN' technique, you will find that listening becomes a lot easier because you are 'buying-out' the time to do it. That said you need to consider how to maximise your use of that time. Active listening actually involves four different elements. These elements are summarised below using the 'FREE' mnemonic as a memory aid.

Figure 12.2: The four elements of active listening

The four elements of active listening

Facts and information
Reading between the lines
Empathy
Evaluation

As a minute-taker you are naturally listening for facts and information. You need to concentrate hard to ensure that you are able to extract the key points from the discussion and any action points. You also need to listen for facts which may need to be included in your summary of the discussion.

You also need to 'listen' for what is not said. Sometimes it is clear that participants mean something different from what they say. Other times it is not so clear, but may still be the case, so listen carefully and learn how to read between the lines. For example, if someone uses the term: 'mature garden' then they probably mean overgrown! Why is this important in minute-taking? Because you need to write *summaries* in the final minutes, you have to effectively capture the 'flavour' of the discussion. If you detect a different meaning behind the word – a subtle nuance – then this will shape your understanding and you should note it. You can then clarify the meaning with the participant concerned after the meeting or, if you're absolutely sure of the real meaning, include it when writing the final minutes.

Listening with empathy is also important. Why are people saying what they are saying? If you can try to see things from their perspective, it will give you greater ability to summarise the point, particularly in meetings where you are required to produce a relatively detailed account. This form of listening can also help you to develop your relationship with the chairperson and the participants. An appreciation of the pressures they may be working under can help you to tailor your approach.

Evaluative listening is vital. This is where you have to decide what is important or not. Under the 'LEARN' technique you are not trying to note everything, so you need to filter information, group it and cross-relate it before selecting the precise information you are going to need in order to write an effective minute.

Some tips for effective listening are given in the following checklist on listening skills.

CHECKLIST

Listening skills

- In meetings, much can be gleaned from what is not said (e.g. the tone of voice or the body language can speak volumes). *Listen* to these messages.
- Remember keen listening will have a positive motivational effect on the *speaker* – who will then be more likely to share information in a positive way. So as a listener, look attentive, show interest and maintain eye contact.
- For important meetings, get a good night's sleep the night before. Tiredness impairs concentration and makes it very hard to listen actively.
- Listen very carefully to the summaries made periodically by the chairperson. You will develop a clear mental picture of how the meeting is progressing.
- Following a period of active listening, make your brief notes of the key points (LEARN). This will assist concentration and aid retention.
- Do not prejudge what a participant is going to say. Listen with an open mind.
- Listen carefully to phraseology not just content. Sometimes phrases can be very descriptive of the way a person is really feeling.
- Always listen respectfully to others; they will then be obliged to accord the same respect to you.
- Check that *your* non-verbal behaviour does not inhibit freeness of expression on the part of the speaker.
- Conduct your personal 'Listening Evaluation'
  - What should I *start to do* to become an active listener?
  - What should I *continue to do* to remain an active listener?
  - What should I *stop doing* in order to become a more effective listener?
- Ask frequent questions to clarify meaning.

> ### CHECKLIST continued
> - When listening, never be rehearsing what *you* are going to say next.
> - If you arrive at the meeting with a mind full of distractions (figurative noise), off-load them before entering the meeting room. This will take a determined mental effort, but you can do nothing about other matters when you are in the meeting room. So, you might as well focus fully on the job at hand and give yourself one less problem!

Summary

This chapter has addressed the importance of understanding the '3Vs' of communication and the need to consider them when evaluating the contributions made by participants and also to bear them in mind when assessing your own communication style. The topic of active listening was examined, with some practical tips provided regarding how to develop active listening skills.

As a proactive minute-taker, there are other personal qualities that you can develop and apply which will increase your credibility in the eyes of others. These are considered in Chapter 13.

13
Personal qualities of the proactive minute-taker

In the previous chapter the importance of the '3Vs' of communication was emphasised. However, demonstrating an effective communication style can be difficult if a person lacks confidence. For example, if a person is nervous it will be reflected in the quality of the voice and in the body language signals conveyed.

In this chapter, a brief consideration is provided of some additional 'soft-skills' topics which can further contribute to the effectiveness of the proactive minute-taker.

As a minute-taker you may sometimes have to battle with misconceptions about the nature of your role and 'fight' to have your opinions heard. Therefore, it is extremely important that you are able to establish credibility in the eyes of others. You can do this in many practical ways (e.g. by being efficient, punctual and accurate). However, the opinion people have of you is also shaped powerfully by the way you *interact* with people and by how *confident* they perceive you to be. This chapter focuses on three specific personal qualities required by proactive minute-takers:

- assertiveness;
- self-confidence; and
- emotional intelligence.

Assertiveness

People tend to equate assertiveness with aggressiveness, or at least with being a little bit 'pushy'. However, this is not the case. Imagine that you booked a full body massage at a top class health club. Consider the following scenarios.

(1) The masseur prepares you for the massage and then proceeds to hit you with his fists repeatedly and then kick you as hard as he can. Will you feel refreshed? Hardly!
(2) This time he simply strokes his little finger softly up and down your back again and again. Will you feel like you've had a good work-out? Very unlikely!
(3) The masseur strokes his fingers up and down your back, but periodically presses the ends of his nails hard into your skin as he is doing so. Will you pay him the money? Very doubtful!
(4) The masseur gently but firmly massages your back, applying just the right amount of pressure to release any tension and relax the muscles. Does that sound more like it? Absolutely!

The approach in the first scenario is totally aggressive. In the second one it is totally passive. The third appears passive, but has aggressive undertones, a sort of passive-aggressive. Only in scenario four is the correct amount of pressure assertively applied to achieve the desired effect.

So, applying this illustration to interpersonal exchanges, an assertive approach is one where a person is confident enough to clearly express what they think in a respectful way, whilst taking into account the rights and feelings of the other person. Consider the following case study.

CASE STUDY

Petros was a member of a team based in the finance department of a large commercial organisation. He was extremely meticulous and paid great attention to detail in his work. Because of this, he built a reputation for being efficient, accurate and reliable. However, Petros was painfully shy by nature and found it hard to express his opinions openly, particularly in situations involving conflict. Because of his reputation for accuracy and efficiency, he was asked by a senior manager to take the minutes at two high-profile meetings: a consultative committee and a management board. He felt nervous but didn't like to say no, so he agreed. At consultative committee meetings individual members were always asking him to make alterations to the draft. He would spend extra time making the changes and cross-checking with everyone that they were happy with them. This became a regular feature of the process: on one occasion, where the meeting had been particularly long and quite contentious, he worked through a public holiday in order to get the minutes finished. At the management board meetings the situation was a little different. Petros found many of the points of discussion hard to understand and felt nervous about interrupting or even talking with the chairperson during the meeting. The chairperson took firm control over the checking of the draft and frequently had to make amendments to the minutes. Petros began to feel frustrated in the role and it began to affect his health. Eventually, he found the courage to discuss the situation with his line manager who arranged for him to be relieved of his minute-taking duties.

Case analysis

The case illustrates why assertiveness is important for the minute-taker. Petros should have made it clear to the committee members that the chairperson was responsible for checking the accuracy of the draft and should have assertively resisted the pressure to continually alter the minutes to satisfy personal whim. In the management board meetings, he should have interrupted when he failed to understand, or at the very least, talked to the chairperson to clarify points. In the end, he wasted precious time and became needlessly stressed, all because he failed to express himself assertively.

All minute-takers need to speak up at a meeting from time to time, to discuss issues with the chairperson and also to speak with participants before and after the meeting. This could be to ask for more information, to clarify areas of misunderstanding or to encourage people to respond to deadlines. So, assertiveness is important.

STOP AND THINK

Take a few minutes to give some thought to the following:

(a) Would you say that you were an assertive person? If the answer is yes, what are the factors which enable you to be so?
(b) If your answer is no, then what do you think is necessary in order for you to be able to cultivate this quality?

Hopefully you were able to identify some key factors in connection with being assertive. There is no easy way to develop this quality, it requires a conscious effort. However, it will be well worth that effort as you gradually discern the benefits.

CHECKLIST

Assertiveness

- Develop your self-confidence; these two areas are very closely related.
- Remember the '3Vs'. Speak clearly and audibly and always maintain good eye contact with the person.
- Remember the visual signals you are conveying. In terms of body language aim to be poised and natural. Stand straight, but do not be too rigid; avoid being overbearing.
- Be clear about the matters you are going to speak about. Even where you are asking for an explanation of a point which you don't understand, you need to able to clearly articulate what it is you want to know.
- Use questions and listen respectfully and actively.
- Demonstrate that you are interested in achieving the best solution for everyone concerned.
- Show personal interest in other people.
- Express appreciation for any assistance provided.
- Even if you find that an exchange is not going as well as you had hoped, never fall back into one of the other modes (e.g. passive or aggressive).
- Be honest, open and factual.
- Never talk over another person.
- Avoid unnecessary displays of emotion and be careful not to berate or accuse.
- Don't 'over talk'. State your point and then allow the person time to formulate their reply.
- Listen to the reply and evaluate it before responding again.
- Prepare for the discussion. Think about possible scenarios which could occur and develop ways to deal with them.
- Be assertive and 'stick to your principles', but avoid being dogmatic.

Self-confidence

It is true that some people are more naturally confident than others and some people do suffer from a lack of self-esteem. However, much can be done to *acquire* confidence and any effort expended in this regard will pay dividends. Note the tips in the following checklist on how to develop greater self-confidence.

> ### CHECKLIST
> **Self-confidence**
>
> - Confidence is related to specific things. So, for example, a person may feel confident about one thing because they are good at it, but unconfident about something else. It is not a case of 'you're either a confident person or you're not'. This means that you can systematically target areas to develop.
> - Knowledge is power. If you know your subject you will feel less threatened and more confident. For example, taking the time to research the subject matter which will be discussed in a meeting and learning any technical terms and jargon will make you feel more confident on the day.
> - Try to be a 'glass half-full' rather than a 'glass half-empty' person.
> - Remember that a problem or setback encountered is not the end; keep working to overcome disappointments.
> - Be proud of your achievements but avoid overconfidence and arrogance which can be just as problematic as a lack of confidence.
> - Have the courage to apologise where something is genuinely your fault but avoid the habit of apologising for things that are not!
> - Prepare well in everything you do. For example, many people hate giving presentations and feel unconfident. However, if they prepare thoroughly they will perform better. In turn this positive outcome will increase their level of confidence for the next presentation.
> - Mentally, try to take the focus away from yourself and concentrate more on what you are trying to achieve.
> - Reflect on situations where you have displayed confidence. What enabled you to display confidence in that situation? Can the learning points from this reflection be applied in another situation?
> - Pay attention to your appearance. If you feel good about yourself, you will naturally feel more confident.
> - Think positively and reflect this in your body language. You are not 'just the minute-taker'; you are a professional in your own right. So don't slouch; 'walk tall', make eye contact and always offer a good firm handshake … not too firm of course!

Emotional intelligence

As a minute-taker you interact with a wide variety of people. These exchanges may not always be as positive as you would like, which can be frustrating. On top of this, you have your own stresses: emotions are not something you leave at home when you come to work!

Over recent decades there has been much interest in the idea of *emotional intelligence* and how it can help you as an individual to maintain self-control, reduce stress levels, improve working relationships and influence others without conflict. In 1990, John Mayer and Peter Salovey defined emotional intelligence as:

> The ability to monitor one's own and other's feelings and emotions, to discriminate among them, and to use this information to guide one's thinking and action.

This work was further developed by Daniel Goleman in his book *Emotional Intelligence: Why It Can Matter More than IQ*. He developed a framework comprising of five elements. A summary of the key points is given below:

Figure 13.1: The five elements of emotional intelligence

Self-awareness
Identifying and understanding your strengths and weaknesses and the way you come across to others. The impact your emotions have on your performance.
Self-regulation
Self-control; acting in a positive way; thinking before you take action.
Motivation
Your commitment to achievement and success; taking the initiative.
Empathy
How well you are able to comprehend other people's views.
Social skills
Communication skills; the ability to relate to other people.

So, emotional intelligence means that you are able to recognise your feelings and those of the people around you and to manage your feelings and also to manage relationships. For you, as a minute-taker, these are positive qualities to develop. In thinking about how effective you are at self-management and relationship management, consider the checklist opposite and then think about areas for personal development.

CHECKLIST

Emotional intelligence

- Do you recognise your own emotions?
- Are you aware of the affect your behaviour has on those you work with?
- Do you understand the factors which underpin your behaviours?
- Do you know how your behaviours are viewed by your colleagues?
- Are you aware of what truly motivates you?
- Do you show initiative?
- Are you a negative person or a positive person?
- How do you feel when things go wrong? Are you 'crushed' in defeat?
- How committed are you to the work you undertake?
- Are you flexible and adaptable in your approach?
- Do you create realistic objectives or do you 'overstretch' yourself?
- Are you able to display self-control? Do you keep your temper in check?
- Can you sense when others are emotionally fragile?
- Do you know what things motivate your colleagues?
- Are you 'in-tune' with the needs of others?
- How well to you react to the concerns of others?
- How effective are you at communicating your feelings?
- Are you open and honest with people?
- Do you offer active support to colleagues who are experiencing problems?
- How good a listener are you?

Summary

It is very clear that to be an effective minute-taker you need to acquire a wide range of skills and personal qualities. This chapter has focused on some of the 'softer' areas. These are no less important than developing note-taking and minute-writing skills and competencies. As the pro-active minute-taker you need to be proficient in all these areas if you are to genuinely establish credibility. At times, you may note deficiencies in your skills and competencies. When this happens you need to take steps to bridge the skills gap. Therefore, the need for personal development is examined in greater detail in Chapter 14.

14
Personal skills development

The expression 'use it or lose it' holds true for many aspects of life. For example, a health-conscious person who jogs every day will accrue certain health benefits over time (e.g. increased lung capacity and a healthy heart rate). However, if they then abandon their regime, these benefits begin to erode. Of course, even if they maintain their exercise programme, a person can always identify areas for further improvement and adjust their approach and schedule accordingly. However, it could be that a person is working hard to maintain a healthy regime but is doing something fundamentally wrong (e.g. using the wrong running shoe) which, in time, could have a negative impact. In the same way, you are practising your skills every time you take the notes at a meeting. However, you may discern some areas for possible improvement. You may even be doing something fundamentally wrong in terms of technique (e.g. trying to write down everything), which may need correcting. The purpose of this short chapter is simply to recommend that you should *make* and *take* opportunities for personal and skills development in the context of the minute-taking role, and to provide you with a few ideas for personal development.

The INFER memory aid

When considering the need to develop certain skills, it is good to think in terms of a personal development process. Figure 14.1 shows a useful mnemonic to help you remember the process which is described in more detail below.

Figure 14.1: The INFER memory aid

> **Personal development process**
>
> **I**dentify
> **N**ote
> **F**inalise
> **E**xecute
> **R**eflect

Identify

The first thing is to identify the skills and/or personal qualities that you want to acquire or develop further. Unfortunately, due to the imposed deadlines and pressures inherent in the role, making the time to reflect on development needs requires a conscious effort. You need to be proactive in this and regularly make time to review your needs.

Note

Make a note of all the various options available to you regarding the areas you have identified for further development. Then select the most appropriate one. There may be a number of interventions that you would like to pursue. Where this is the case, create a plan to incorporate them all over a period of time.

Finalise

When you know what you want to do, take steps to finalise the arrangements. You need to be proactive here and avoid procrastination – many a good idea remains just that: a good *idea*!

Execute

Undertake the development intervention (e.g. by attending a training course, reading a book, meeting with an experienced colleague to get tips and advice etc). If, for some reason, you are *unable* to follow through on your plan, don't just place the intervention on the 'back-burner', re-schedule it straightaway.

Reflect

After you have undertaken the development intervention, reflect on what you have learned and take steps to apply these learning points in your role. Monitor how this is working in terms of performance improvement and, if necessary, identify areas of refinement and/or further areas for improvement.

You may find it useful to create a template for a *personal development plan*. This will help you to focus on what you need to do and to plan for it accordingly. The plan should highlight the *issue* giving rise to the development need, the *problem* which is being caused (or could potentially be caused if not addressed), the *action* you intend to take and the *timeframe* for completion.

An example of a suggested template is shown on the following page. This, of course, is only an example. You will need to develop your own structure and approach. Include whatever information you feel will be of practical value to you. It is always a good idea to put your plans in writing as it provides a clear reference point and helps to maintain your focus.

In the model, an example is given regarding how to complete the plan. The timeframe section should reflect your intended 'window' for completion. You may be able to be quite specific here (e.g. if you *know* the exact date of a training course then write it in the plan). However, it is a good idea to make entries on the plan as soon as you identify the issue. Therefore (as in the example given), the exact timings may not be known so you will need to insert a time range in the column. When this is the case, ensure that you are proactive in finalising the arrangements otherwise the opportunity may pass you by. Also, ensure you enter the exact date as soon as it is known.

A personal development plan

Issue	Problem	Action	Timeframe
I am very new to the minute-taking role and have had no formal training. I am unsure of the range of skills and competencies which are required	If the issue is not addressed, I may struggle to complete all necessary tasks with accuracy	*Action one* To meet with one of my colleagues who is an experienced minute-taker and to ask for advice about the best way to perform the role	Within the next week
		Action two To book a place on a minute-taking course (external provider)	Within the next three months

The choice of development initiatives will of course be down to you. Sometimes this might involve a major intervention such as attendance on a training course but, at other times, the initiative could simply involve talking to an experienced colleague or even just mentally acknowledging the need to change an attitude or behaviour. The following checklist provides a series of questions which you could ask yourself to prompt ideas for development initiatives:

CHECKLIST

Self-development: prompting questions

- How effective is my listening?
- Do I have a tendency to write too much?
- Am I able to identify the key points from a discussion with ease?
- Do I always meet my own deadlines?
- What do others say about the quality of my minutes?
- Would I benefit from trying alternative minute-taking techniques?
- Have I got a clear system for structuring my notes?
- Could I be more proficient in my use of technology?

CHECKLIST continued

- Do I prepare thoroughly for all meetings?
- Do I have a well-structured notebook?
- Do I have a reasonable grasp of the subject matter at each of my meetings?
- Have I created my strategy file for each of the meetings I minute?
- Do I fully understand the procedures at all of the meetings I minute?
- Do I clearly understand the meeting cycle for each of the meetings I minute?
- How extensive is my vocabulary?
- Do I make a lot of grammatical mistakes?
- Do I struggle to create cohesive summaries?
- Are my minutes always accurate?
- Are my minutes always clear?
- Do I struggle to find the right phrases when linking parts of the discussion?
- Overall, are my minutes concise?
- Do I clearly document all decisions and actions?
- Do I procrastinate?
- Am I a team player?
- Do I always arrive at meetings on time?
- Am I assertive?
- Am I confident?
- Am I self-controlled?
- How well do I manage relationships?
- Am I interested in other people?
- Do I talk to participants at meetings?
- Do I interrupt to seek clarifications?
- Do I get overly stressed?
- Do I have credibility?
- How effectively do I make use of my voice?
- Does my body language signal a positive message?
- How effective is my relationship with the chairperson (at each meeting)?
- If I contribute and take minutes; how effectively do I balance the two roles?
- Who do I consider to be a good example of an effective minute-taker?
- Why do I consider them to be a good example?

Asking yourself questions like the ones above, will stimulate your thinking about areas which may require improvement. Some aspects will be relatively easy to address whereas others – particularly in the case of an ingrained bad habit – will require development over a period of time. There are many ways and methods by which you can address the issues; a few ideas are given below:

- formal training interventions (e.g. booking on a training course);
- reading specific background material;
- practice sessions;
- talking with an experienced colleague;

- observing an experienced colleague;
- personal reflection resulting in a decision to adjust your approach; and
- asking for specific feedback and applying the suggestions.

The above are just a few ideas and sometimes one particular method can be used to address a number of personal development issues (e.g. training programmes can cover a wide range of topics: minute-taking skills, time management, assertiveness, emotional intelligence etc). Practice sessions can be developed in many areas (e.g. note-taking techniques, listening, summarising etc). Select the methods that work best for you and you will enjoy your personal development journey!

Practice exercises for note-taking

Taking notes is a key part of the minute-taking process. The active development of skills in this area can make a significant difference to the quality of the notes you take in the meeting and, by extension, the quality of the final minutes. Therefore, this final section briefly addresses some approaches you could take to master the necessary skills.

The 'LEARN' technique as advocated in this book will definitely make the entire process of taking the minutes far more effective. However, for some people, it may be a departure from the approach they have been using, perhaps for many years, and there may, understandably, be a fear of trying something new. Is this true in your case? If it is *then practice is* important. The idea of listening first and evaluating the discussion before writing anything, may cause you concern at first. Also, you may be unsure if you will be able to move away from the habit of taking detailed notes towards a more bullet point-based abbreviated style. In order to address this, think of ways that you can practice the art of note-taking in a 'safe environment'.

A good way to do this is to take opportunities for practice *outside* the work environment. One suggestion is to watch a discussion or debate programme on the television and use this as your basis for experiment. Talk shows or political debate programmes are particularly useful for this exercise. First, record part of the discussion (10–20 minutes). Second, play it back; listen for a period of time without taking notes and mentally evaluate the main message. Third, at an appropriate point take down your notes of the key points using short phrases. Finally, play it back and self-assess your performance. How easy was it to do? Did you experience any problems? Did you achieve accuracy? Did you manage to isolate the main message and key points? How would you change your approach if you were to attempt it again? There are many programmes like this on the television so you can repeat the exercise as often as you like! The more you practice, the more efficient you will become.

Short phrases can be shortened even further through the use of abbreviations. A good way to acquire comfort with use of abbreviations is to take opportunities to develop them, again, outside the work environment. Text messaging is a useful tool for doing this: be creative and develop as many abbreviations as you can; the message may be completely unintelligible at the other end, but you will have developed your skills!

When you feel reasonably comfortable with the 'LEARN' technique, move on to applying it in the workplace. Perhaps begin by applying it in an informal meeting first (e.g. a team briefing) where you will feel a little more comfortable. When you decide to apply it for the first time in a formal meeting, you could think about the use of a *smartpen* (see Chapter 11). This would provide you with a 'safety net' and allow you to practice the technique without worrying about something going wrong.

Summary

For the proactive minute-taker, skills development is important. There are many facets to the role and there are a number of 'hard' and 'soft' skills which need to be applied if you are to be truly effective. Hopefully, by reading through the prompting questions above you will be able to generate some meaningful areas for self-development. Remember, of course, to document your ideas in a personal development plan. This will serve to 'formalise' the process and add focus to your objectives.

Final thoughts

Whether you've read this book from cover to cover or simply accessed the chapters that interest you the most, we sincerely hope that you've enjoyed it and been able to isolate many practical points for personal application. We would certainly encourage you to keep it handy on the bookshelf and refer to it often as you continue on your valiant journey!

Our aim when writing the book was to provide a comprehensive overview of the minute-taking process from the perspective of the minute-taker. Over the years, we at TMF Training have – in conjunction with ICSA – worked with literally hundreds of minute-takers from a wide range of organisations in both the public and private sectors and we have tried to reflect as many of their views, suggestions and concerns as possible in the material we have presented.

We have always been struck by the sheer professionalism of the minute-takers we have worked with and their Herculean efforts to produce excellent quality minutes despite the, often unprofessional, level of support they receive. Many wrestle with definitional vagueness about the nature of their role, their perceived lack of status in the eyes of some, poorly organised and chaired meetings, sometimes difficult, awkward and uncommunicative participants, unreasonable demands and impossible deadlines and yet still they battle on!

The overriding message of this book is that the successful minute-taker is a *proactive* minute-taker. This necessitates building the confidence to take control and push for change when it is in the interests of achieving a more effective minute-taking process for all concerned. It will involve challenging convention and culture, working hard to establish meaningful professional relationships with both the chairperson and the participants for each meeting and taking the initiative for personal skills development.

We firmly believe that adopting a proactive stance over time will result in achieving greater professional recognition within your organisation and that the overall minute-taking experience will become far more rewarding and, dare we say, enjoyable!

So, minute-takers, we salute you! We can surely do no better than to conclude with an adaptation of the old Chinese proverb:

> If you want to be happy for a day, get drunk. If you want to be happy for a week, get married. If you want to be happy for life, become a minute-taker!

Appendix 1
Troubleshooter

It is very much hoped that by reading this book you have had many of your questions and concerns frequently answered! Of course, minute-taking seems to continually throw up new challenges and everyone's experience is different. The issues that you face in carrying out your role will depend to an extent on the nature and culture of your organisation, your own experience and level of self-confidence, the attitude of the people you work alongside and the parameters of your own job role.

This book has been aimed at a broad readership. It is hoped that whatever type of organisation you work in and whatever the nature of the meetings you minute, you have been able to find many points which you can either apply directly, or adapt to your own specific requirements.

The purpose of this appendix is to address a range of questions frequently asked by minute-takers. Of course, they may not necessarily be the questions that *you* frequently ask! That said, the aim is to explore some varied areas and hopefully there will be something here for everyone. The following questions are presented in no particular order and feature a mix of personal, organisational and legal issues:

Is it ever necessary to record a contribution word-for-word, where brevity in minute-taking is the accepted norm?

Yes it is. Consider the following scenario: At a board meeting, one of the directors disagrees vehemently with a decision taken; however he is the only person dissenting, all the other directors (i.e. the majority) are in agreement. The board has not taken a formal vote, but the stand taken by the director is firm and he asks that his expression of dissent be recorded. In effect, this really represents a vote against the resolution. Because of the evidential nature of minutes, the director concerned will be keen to protect himself from any liability which may arise from the decision taken. Therefore, the minutes should record such requests with clarity.

There may be a variety of other reasons why people request that a detailed record be included in the minutes regarding something that was said. You will need to assess each case on its own merits. Always consult the chairperson if in doubt. However, very detailed or word-for-word recording should be the exception and not the rule.

What can I do if the chairperson or other contributors change the contents of my minutes, thereby affecting their accuracy?

The answer to the following question makes clear the situation regarding alterations to the minutes *after* they have been signed. However, what about requests received prior to that point? The minute taker has a duty to record accurately. Usually, if there is a different view by the chairperson of how a minute should be drafted, a compromise can be reached. However, if there is a fundamental disagreement in the wording, it needs to be resolved when the minutes are agreed at the next meeting. For example, you might say: 'I recorded this; the chairperson wants it to say this - how does the meeting want it recorded?' If you disagree on a serious matter, or if you are asked to do something which you know to be illegal, then you must refer the issue to the appropriate authority within the organisation or back to the next meeting. It is unlikely that this will occur very often, if at all. Most of the time, you can safely accept the chairperson's decision.

What should I do if I am asked to change the minutes after they have been signed by the chairperson?

You should not make any changes to the minutes after they have been signed by the chairperson. Any details which were not available at the meeting itself must not be inserted in the minutes. What, then, can be done? Taking the situation regarding companies as an example, note the following quote by Andrew Hamer from *The ICSA Meetings and Minutes Handbook*:

> If the directors present at a subsequent meeting disagree with a decision taken at a previous meeting that is properly recorded in signed minutes, they should pass a further resolution rescinding or amending their previous decision which should be recorded in the minutes of that meeting. Similarly, if it is discovered after the minutes have been signed that they are inaccurate, a further resolution should be passed and recorded in the minutes of the meeting at which the inaccuracy was raised.

If an argument breaks out, should I minute it?

Well the first thing to remember is not to join in! The eruption of an argument can be emotionally destabilising for all concerned, so maintain your composure and focus. However, there is no value in minuting the actual argument; the exchange will be loaded with emotionally charged expressions which have no place in the final minutes. However, you should make a note of the point that was being discussed for your own reference. It is the chairperson's responsibility to bring the meeting back to order; allow that to happen and then – when order has been restored – recommence your note-taking activities.

Is it always bad practice to include details regarding the opinions given and emotions displayed by the contributors?

It is not appropriate to include strong opinions, deeply held personal views, cynical comments, angry tirades and expressions of frustration in the final set of minutes. Minutes need to remain *objective*. Note the learning point from the following case study.

> ### CASE STUDY
>
> A new IT system was being introduced at XYZ Ltd. A firm of IT consultants had been hired to manage the implementation in conjunction with the in-house IT department. The project had not been going well and time slippages were occurring. There were even concerns that the project was running into serious financial trouble. Project team meetings were attended by representatives of XYZ senior management and project team personnel. The lead consultant Barry and the IT manager Mike, were regular attenders. At the next project team meeting, Barry was unable to attend. The regular minute taker was also unable to attend, so a stand-in was recruited for the job. When the apologies were read out and Barry's name was mentioned, Mike the IT manager said: 'That just goes to show doesn't it? As far as I'm concerned, Barry is completely divorced from this process both physically and mentally!' The minute-taker faithfully recorded every word in his notes. However, he also faithfully recorded exactly the same words in the final minutes! The chairperson failed to scrutinise the minutes for possible amendments and they were dispatched by the minute-taker to all members of the group. Not surprisingly, Barry was none too pleased! The result was a major argument between Barry and Mike at a time when team cohesion was required like never before.

Although the names have been changed, this actually happened. Oh, the power of a few ill-chosen words! So, always be very careful to keep your minutes as objective as possible. This does not mean that expressions of concern can never be noted; in some cases it may be appropriate to do so and some minutes will naturally be more detailed than others. In the case of a joint consultative committee meeting for example, it may be acceptable for certain views and opinions to be recorded. If ever in doubt, discuss the matter with the chairperson.

Is it always best to use the passive voice when writing minutes?

Not necessarily. Although this is the approach that has been featured in this book this is not because there are no viable alternatives; it is because this is the traditional approach to minute writing which many organisations employ. However, there are also many organisations where a more active style is preferred. This is perfectly acceptable. You should always follow the conventions in your particular organisation. The key point to remember of course is that whichever style you choose you must be consistent.

What is the procedure if the chairperson deals with an agenda item in a different order from the printed agenda?

The agenda provides the guide or 'road-map' for the meeting but, just as on a literal journey, you may occasionally be required to deviate from the original course, so the order of the agenda items may sometimes need to change. This is not a problem in itself, but you need to be careful that you adopt the correct approach for the minutes. The minutes should be written to reflect the way the meeting actually happened. So, if, for example, agenda item 10 is now going to be dealt with just after agenda item 3, then it now becomes agenda item 4. When you follow this approach, the real 'shape' of the meeting is preserved. However, there are some times when this convention is not followed, for example, when discussion on two linked issues has to be split for a particular administrative reason, but the minutes make better sense if the items are minuted together.

For companies, do any particular measures need to be taken in order to guard against the possible falsification of minutes?

Companies need to be vigilant in this regard. If the minutes are kept in minute books, various protective measures could be taken. For example, the book should be stored in a safe place with limits on who can gain access. The chairperson should initial every page, there should be sequential numbering for each type of meeting and binders should be used which are capable of being locked. It is also advisable to use separate books for board meetings and general meetings. Members have the right to inspect the minutes of general meetings, but board minutes and minutes relating to management meetings should not be made available to members.

There could be legal problems if appropriate measures are not taken. It is far easier to *challenge* the content of the minutes where it can be shown that effective security measures were not in place.

For companies, how should minutes be retained?

The following extracts are reproduced from The Law and Practice of Company Meetings by Andrew Hamer. All references to 'the Act' are to the Companies Act 2006. All statutory references are to the relevant section number of the Companies Act 2006.

Minutes were traditionally handwritten in bound books kept for that purpose. Although it is still perfectly acceptable to record minutes in this manner, it is far more likely that minutes will be produced as a print-out of a word-processor file (or less commonly these days, typed on sheets of paper). Where bound books are still used, the print-out or typed-up copy of the minutes can then be pasted in the serially numbered pages of the bound minute book.

Minute books specifically designed for purpose often include pages that allow an index to be created. Many company secretaries use these to index the minutes by subject and names mentioned. Although there is no legal requirement to do this, it is considered good practice and will be particularly helpful when it is necessary to refer, for example, to decisions of the directors which have the effect of modifying the company's articles.

Many companies now use loose-leaf minute books. Although this is allowed under the Act, additional precautions must be taken to guard against falsification as they are not bound books. If a loose-leaf minute book is used, it is preferable (but not essential) to use one which has a locking device either in the spine or between the covers. Strict control should be exercised over access to the keys to the minute book and any duplicates should be lodged in a secure place such as a safe or safety deposit box. When a loose-leaf folder is used, the pages should be serially numbered at the time of insertion in the binder, normally under the control of the secretary or the person acting as the secretary to the relevant body. The items minuted are also usually numbered consecutively from one meeting to the next so as to prevent the insertion of a false set of minutes.

All minute books, whether bound books or loose-leaf folders, should be kept in a secure place. Ideally this should be a robust, lockable and fireproof filing cabinet or safe to which access is restricted. This is of even greater importance if minutes are kept in an ordinary unlockable, loose-leaf folder.

One would normally expect the minutes of meetings to be entered in the minute books in date order, and the appearance of any minutes out of order could give rise to questions as to their veracity should the minute book ever need to be tendered as evidence in legal proceedings.

If minutes are kept in electronic form they must still be authenticated by the chairman to be treated as evidence of the proceedings under s. 249 (minutes of directors' meetings) or s. 356 (minutes of general meetings and records of resolutions). Any doubts over the admissibility of electronic signatures in legal proceedings for these purposes have been removed by the Electronic Communications Act 2000. Accordingly, the chairman could apply an electronic signature to a file containing the minutes which could then be stored on a computer. As the security of the technique used to apply the electronic signature could have a bearing on the weight the courts give to the minutes, it would be preferable for the chairman to use the most modern cryptographic techniques to do this.

Different considerations arise where it is proposed, for example, to scan manually signed minutes for retention in computerised form and to destroy the original paper copies. Where this is done, the electronic image may ultimately need to be tendered in evidence in court, as secondary evidence of the signature of the minutes and of their contents. To ensure that it is acceptable as evidence in this regard, it will be essential to follow the British Standards Institute's Code of Practice for Legal Admissibility of Information Stored Electronically.

If minutes are kept in computerised form, they must still be capable of being reproduced in hard copy form (s. 1135(2)). This probably sounds simpler than it is in reality. The minutes must still be capable of being reproduced in hard copy form not just today but for at least ten years (or indefinitely if they are 1985 Act records). Ideally, whenever a new computer system or new software is adopted, checks should be carried out to ensure that the files containing the minutes can still be read. If not, it may be possible to convert them into a suitable format. However, if this is not possible (e.g. because doing so would compromise the electronic signature), it may be necessary to retain the old hardware and software forever. These considerations will obviously be less of a problem for minutes and records kept under the 2006 Act regarding meetings and decisions made on or after 1 October 2007 as these only have to be kept for ten years. Nevertheless, many companies will probably wish to keep these records for longer than the ten-year minimum prescribed by the Act.

I know it is a good idea to use bullet points when taking the notes, but is it appropriate to use bullet points in the actual written minutes?

You can use bullet points in the written minutes but think carefully why you are using them. Think back to the 'eight Cs' of the minute-taking mix introduced in Chapter 1. Accurate minutes should be clear. Bullet points can be an aid to clarity if they are used to break up a large body of text and present a list of points under a particular theme. For example, if you are discussing the advantages and disadvantages of something, simple bullet point lists can make the points stand out more clearly than incorporating all the words into a sentence. However, be careful with presentation. The final minutes are not the vehicle for experimenting with as many bullet point styles as you can! Also, be careful to not overuse them. Think of them more as the icing on the cake, not the cake itself!

I have a tendency to take very detailed notes at the meeting and I've done this for years. No one has ever complained about the quality of my minutes so why should I change now?

This is an interesting question because a lot of minute-takers feel this way. If you are one of them, think why no one has ever complained. It is probably because you are a consummate professional who works hard to produce the perfect minutes every time. So, the argument for making a change in approach and learning to write less is that it will benefit *you*. It may be that in producing your minutes you are investing more time than is required at the note-structuring stage. Also, you are probably working harder than you need to during the meeting trying to keep pace with the discussion. If you practice and then apply the 'LEARN' technique as advocated in this book, you will have all the information you need to produce that perfect set of minutes, but you will feel far less fatigued when leaving the meeting room and you will definitely save yourself some time at the minute-writing stage.

Minute-taking can be a demanding activity. Surely it makes sense to apply job rotation principles and share the task?

This is a fair question. Minute-takers throughout the land would no doubt leap for joy if this idea was to become standard practice! On the face of it, such an arrangement is certainly feasible but, if it is to work, some issues need to be considered:

- Regular minute-takers work hard to develop a relationship with the chairperson and this can take some time. If the chairperson is continually exposed to different minute-takers, establishing effective working relationships could be challenging.
- Each minute-taker needs to acquire the same understanding regarding the subject matter discussed at the meetings.
- Performance standards may vary between minute-takers, thus creating possible friction and bad feeling.

- Minute-taking is more of an art than a science and minute-takers put their own 'stamp' on their work. Problems may arise if the final minutes show too much variation in style between different minute-takers.
- The minute-taking team need to establish a healthy team ethic and be prepared to share information and support one another.

If the above issues can be satisfactorily addressed, then it may be possible to develop a workable job rotation scheme.

Who should take the minutes at board meetings?

Ideally, it should be the company secretary (ICSA's *Code on Good Boardroom Practice*; the Cadbury Report, para. 4.25). However, minutes can also be taken by the assistant or deputy secretary. It *is* possible for others to take the minutes but because objectivity is important, care needs to be exercised in this regard. Of course, company secretaries do more than take the minutes. An important part of their function is to advise the board on various matters during the meeting. For this reason, the company secretary may appoint an assistant to provide help in recording the proceedings.

If the minutes are going to be accessible to those outside the meeting (i.e. employees of the organisation in general and perhaps members of the public) are there any safeguards that I need to consider?

Care needs to be taken that the minutes do not reveal information which should be kept confidential and the minutes need to be worded in such a way that the organisation is not placed in a bad light. Think carefully about the timing of releasing the minutes to general view. It would obviously be a mistake to release a draft version before any amendments had been made.

Should minutes be published and if so, what may be the impact on content and style?

The following information is taken from ICSA's recently published guidance document with regard to effective minute taking. This guidance is the product of ICSA's discussions with experienced minute takers, from both corporate and not-for-profit sectors:

> *Some organisations such as public bodies and regulators choose – or are obliged – to provide complete transparency over their board meetings by publishing board papers and minutes on their websites. However, it has been suggested that this level of transparency might result in the board meetings ceasing to be the decision-making body for the organisation, with confidential or 'water cooler' meetings held separately from board meetings to discuss matters and agree a position, before the matter is 'discussed' by the board and made public.*

In a similar vein, a number of organisations, particularly in the public sector have an obligation to respond to Freedom of Information requests, which may require the publication of minutes.

This is an area in which we found a sharp divergence between the corporate responses and those of some public sector entities, with the former firmly against publication and the latter largely in favour. To some extent, the public sector view may be swayed by the fact that a number of organisations are required to publish minutes by their constitutions or other relevant regulations, but in the corporate sector board meetings and their minutes are seen as a private matter.

Arguments in favour of publication tended to emphasise transparency and openness, and at least one respondent saw this as a more modern approach. However, there was a very strong opposing view that, in addition to the issues of commercial sensitivity and confidentiality associated with publishing minutes, publication would actually undermine transparency by impeding open discussion in board meetings and by adversely affecting the quality of the minutes. It would create a risk that significant decisions would be taken outside the board meeting and that minutes would be written with publication in mind.

Where there are legislative or regulatory requirements for board minutes to be published, that must, of course, be done. However, where there are no such requirements, it seems to us that the disadvantages are likely to outweigh the advantages although individual organisations are free to make their own decision based on their own circumstances.

There are important differences, too, between the level of risk associated with the publication of minutes and response to requests under the FOIA. This is because requests under FOIA are generally more limited in impact – either because the information requested is more specific and exemptions apply to what must be provided, or because it is being provided to a limited audience rather than being published on a website available worldwide.

This is another issue where organisations will need to come to their own decision, and we do not feel it appropriate to give guidance. The Information Commissioner already provides detailed guidance for those organisations which are obliged to publish minutes and those seeking to do so voluntarily should, in our view, seek specific legal advice.

So, where minutes *are* to be published, the choices made in terms of style and content will necessarily reflect the circumstances of the particular organisation. Some organisations, for example, draft a report from the board that uses the minutes as a basis - but avoids confidential items. Also, with regard to the *focus* of minutes according to the type of organisation, the following extract from the ICSA's guidance document is worthy of note:

For example, a charity or public sector organisation may focus more on ensuring there is clear accountability visible through the minutes, in some cases having consideration of the fact that the minutes will be in the public domain. Alternatively, a regulated financial services company is more likely to focus on providing evidence of robust decision making; demonstrating that directors undertook their duties and responsibilities in accordance with both statutory and regulatory requirements and gave matters, particularly those relating to risk, appropriate consideration.

Is it permissible for the chairperson to take the minutes?

It may be permissible, but it is not advisable. In some relatively informal meetings where the minutes are really just a brief set of action points, then the chairperson could undertake the role without too many problems. However, for more formal meetings such a practice is not recommended. The role of the chairperson is a demanding one and if an attempt is made to take notes of the proceedings *and* chair the meeting, it is almost inevitable that both jobs will be performed unsatisfactorily.

Are there occasions where I may need to record a little more detail than usual in the minutes?

This could be the case. Sometimes decisions are reached after a very long and intense period of debate characterised by strong emotive argument and forceful expressions of opinion. Objectivity should always be maintained, so although it would be bad practice to record the intensity of the discussion, it might be the course of wisdom to include some extra detail to reflect that both sides of the argument had been fully considered before arriving at the decision.

Consider another example. An important strategic decision has been taken following considerable discussion relating to a number of possible scenarios. The debate has been both constructive and objective and a consensus decision has been reached. However, it may still be a good idea to provide more detail in the minutes than just the final decision. Perhaps a brief summary of the reasons *why* the other scenarios were rejected could be provided. The reason for this is because the decision was a particularly important one and the minutes can provide the evidence that all possible options were considered before the final selection: the choice was not made rashly or in haste.

Another example would be where the subject matter is of a particularly sensitive nature and the final decision is likely to affect some individuals in a negative way. Here, the minutes may need to provide extra detail to clearly demonstrate that the subject was debated fully prior to reaching the decision. Also, there are times when some of the content of a background report needs to go into the minutes – particularly on very substantive items; for example, if legal advice has been sought and this is considered, it is often a good idea to say this as it shows the reasonableness of a decision.

As a minute-taker, I feel I have low status at some of the meetings I minute. Why is this?

This is a common feeling amongst minute-takers and a point which is often raised and discussed at minute-taking courses. Sometimes the problem lies with the minute-taker, who may feel this way because they lack self-confidence. It can be quite an ordeal for some people to enter a room full of people they don't know and who hold 'high-powered' jobs. They feel like an outsider. Sometimes the feeling of low status is reinforced in the mind of the minute-taker by the behaviour of the participants, who may feel that they are the important 'players' in the meeting because they are the 'experts'; the minute-taker is only there to take the notes. Although such people may not be overtly rude, they communicate their disinterest through their body language and failure to acknowledge the minute-taker. Some participants appreciate neither the importance of the minute-taking task nor the high level of skills and competency required to carry it out effectively – there is a lack of acknowledgement of the minute-taker as a fellow professional. This attitude is particularly noticeable where the minute-taker is of 'lower rank' in the organisational hierarchy.

If you feel this way, you will not be able to alter perceptions overnight, but you can do much to improve the situation if you work to establish your credibility. This book is full of suggestions, tips and ideas on how to be proactive and fulfil your role in a professional way. If you apply these points and carry out all your duties in a professional manner, then you will have done as much as you can and you will draw a measure of personal satisfaction from this. If some people continue to see your role as a low status function, the problem lies with them, not you.

In some management meetings, presentations are given. Is it necessary to minute these? If it is, are there any guidelines to help me minute them effectively?

In many cases it will not be necessary to minute presentations. For example, a paper-based summary of the presentation and/or a copy of the slides may have been attached to the agenda or tabled on the day. In such cases the minute should simply note that the presentation was given, by whom and on what topic.

Sometimes however, a discussion session takes place following the presentation. In such cases, it may be necessary to provide *some* detail relating to the points made in the discussion.

On occasion, you may be asked to summarise a presentation in the minutes even where a handout has been provided. This can occur where the presentation relates to an important issue and it is decided that it needs to be summarised in the written record of the meeting. In such cases it is likely that a discussion session will follow and that certain decisions may be taken. The discussion part can be summarised in the same way that you would summarise any other discussion (i.e. emphasising the main message and any decisions and actions taken). The summary of the presentation which precedes it should provide a succinct overview. When summarising a presentation, you need to highlight its purpose, the key points developed and any conclusions drawn or recommendations made. It is also a good idea to ask the presenter to check your final summary. The quality of delivery in some presentations can be poor and it's important that you capture the true essence of what the speaker was trying to convey.

With regard to companies, how long should minutes be retained for?

With regard to minutes of directors' meetings, the Companies Act 2006, s. 248(2) states: 'the records must be kept for at least 10 years from the date of the meeting'. With regard to records of resolutions and meetings etc, s. 355 states:

(1) Every company must keep records comprising:
   (a) copies of all resolutions of members passed otherwise than at general meetings;
   (b) minutes of all proceedings of general meetings; and
   (c) details provided to the company in accordance with section 357 (decisions of sole member).
(2) The records must be kept for at least ten years from the date of the resolution, meeting or decision (as appropriate).

However, this ten-year retention period only applies to records in respect of meetings held, resolutions passed or decisions made on or after 1 October 2007. Regarding decisions made prior to this date, minutes and related records must be retained permanently (Companies Act 1985 applies).

Notwithstanding the provisions of the 2006 Act, taking into account the evidential nature of minutes and the fact that they form a valuable historical record, it would be wise to retain the records on a permanent basis.

As a minute-taker, am I responsible for ensuring that the actions agreed at the meeting are completed?

Minute-takers seem to get a raw deal at times: at one end of the scale they're expected to make the coffee and at the other end they're expected to 'hunt down' action takers and force them to fulfil their promises! It is really the chairperson's job to do this. As the minute-taker you can hardly be expected to be responsible for ensuring that, for example, a senior manager completes an agreed action. However, some minute-takers *are* expected to be progress chasers. This is not necessarily a bad thing because it maintains your profile as the proactive minute-taker and encourages people to meet deadlines. However, it is important that the chairperson realises that your role is purely to follow up on progress and give reminders to people; you are not responsible for ensuring that the actions have been completed.

I'm new to the minute-taking role and feel that I don't have the necessary skills to cope. I always seem to struggle, what can I do?

New minute-takers can find the overall experience somewhat overwhelming. If you are struggling, don't be too quick to conclude that you are not cut out for the role. Skills development is very important in this job and it is unfortunate that many organisations fail to provide any initial training for new minute-takers. Therefore, you are warmly encouraged to take special note of all the points made in Chapter 14 on personal skills development and to be proactive in acquiring all the skills you need to perform your role effectively.

Appendix 2
Checklists

In Chapter 5, you were encouraged to develop a specific strategy for each meeting you minute, involving all the necessary activities which need to be carried out before, during and after the meeting.

Here we provide you with three detailed checklists. These are designed as reminder tools that provide a bullet-point reference guide to help you in ensuring that all essential activities have been undertaken. The checklists are presented as a series of prompting questions and cover:

- issues to be considered *before* the meeting;
- issues to be considered *during* the meeting; and
- issues to be considered *after* the meeting.

It is recognised, of course, that the scope and scale of the minute-taking role varies considerably between different practitioners and you may find that some of the points highlighted do not apply to you. Conversely, you may find that you have more to add! In any event, they will stimulate your thinking and could act as a useful start point for developing your minute-taking strategy in line with the ideas in Chapter 5.

Before you begin scanning the lists, please remember the following with respect to each one:

The 'before' list

This list covers a wide range of activities in connection with pre-meeting preparation. You should review this list *well in advance*; some of the activities require a longer lead-time for completion, whereas others will relate to activities on the day of the meeting itself.

The 'during' list

This list covers all the points which need to be considered in relation to the meeting itself. However, it is unlikely that you will be sitting in the meeting attempting to take the notes while at the same time pondering the contents of the reminder checklist! So, the best approach is to consider the points prior to the meeting as a form of preparation and then review them again following the meeting as a form of evaluation. In time, the points will become well embedded in your mind and you will naturally reflect on some of these points *during* the meetings you minute.

The 'after' list

This list covers all the activities which follow the meeting. Some relate to activities which should be undertaken straight after the meeting, some to the writing of the actual minutes and others to self-development activities and self-reflection. The conclusions you draw from your review of this list will naturally feed in to your preparation activities for the meeting that follows.

CHECKLIST

The minute-taker's reminder checklist: Before the meeting

Tick the following as completed:
- Do I clearly understand the meeting cycle for this meeting?
- Have I created a timeline plan to show how this meeting cycle dovetails with those for the other meetings I attend?
- Am I expected to contribute at this meeting in addition to taking the minutes?
- If I am expected to contribute for one item only, have I made arrangements for someone else to take the minutes for that one item?
- If I am expected to be the minute taker and full meeting contributor, have I explained to everyone that the minutes will be more concise than usual with the emphasis on noting action points? Have I explained to the chairperson that a summary would be appreciated at the end of each item?
- Am I fully aware of the layout and style of the minutes required in respect of this meeting?
- Do I fully understand all the procedural matters in relation to this particular meeting?
- Have I confirmed all the necessary administration arrangements for the meeting?
- Have I checked that all equipment is in good working order?
- Has the meeting room been arranged in the way the participants have requested?
- Have I read thoroughly the minutes of the last meeting?
- Have I read and fully understood the agenda?
- Have I read and understood all the supporting papers?
- Is there any additional information that I need to read and understand in order to be fully prepared?
- If I need help, what should my approach be for this particular meeting?
  - Speak to the participant(s) before the day?
  - Speak to the participant(s) before the meeting?
  - Speak to the chair in advance of the meeting?
  - Seek clarifications afterwards?
  - Talk to the chair during the meeting?
  - Interrupt during the meeting?
- Have I copied all the necessary papers for the meeting, including the minutes of the last meeting?
- Do I have enough copies?
- Is the chair required to sign the minutes? Do I have a copy for this purpose?
- With respect to this meeting, do I know who the chair is?

CHECKLIST continued

- If I have not worked with the chair before, what can I do to establish a professional relationship?
- Have I arranged a pre-meeting briefing session with the chair?
- If a briefing is not possible prior to the day of the meeting, have I arranged for a short discussion with the chair just prior to the commencement of the meeting?
- Have I made arrangements to sit next to the chair at the meeting?
- If it is not possible to sit next to the chair what arrangements can I make to ensure that the quality of my note-taking is not compromised?
- Have I created an attendance list for circulation at the meeting?
- Is all my paperwork well arranged and in good order?
- Have I created a minute-taking template that I am comfortable with?
- If I am using loose-leaf sheets of A4, have I numbered the pages in advance?
- Do I have enough spare writing paper?
- Have I noted all the abbreviations, technical terms and jargon that may be used by participants at this meeting?
- Do I have all the pens and pencils I need including a choice of colours?
- Do I have my highlighter pens?
- Have I allocated time to undertake an initial review of my notes immediately following the meeting?
- Have I arranged to arrive a little earlier at the venue to check the final arrangements and converse with participants?
- Is my personal appearance appropriate for this particular meeting occasion; is it professional?
- Is my clothing comfortable?
- Have I eaten foods that will help to maintain my energy and concentration levels throughout the meeting?
- Have I brought a bottle of water to help maintain hydration levels?
- If I need to interrupt for clarifications, have I practiced my voice projection and assertiveness techniques to enable me to do so with confidence?
- HAVE I PREPARED A PERSONAL CHECKLIST FOR ALL THE ABOVE POINTS?

CHECKLIST

The minute-taker's reminder checklist: during the meeting

Tick the following as completed:

- Have I entered the room confidently?
- Does my body language give evidence that I am a professional person with every right to be at the meeting, in order to fulfil an extremely important role, or does it suggest that I am a second-class citizen who is attending the meeting only to perform the onerous task of note-taking?
- Have I taken the opportunity to mix and converse with participants in order to build rapport?
- Have I placed my papers on the table and arranged my working space in a neat and orderly fashion?
- Have I spoken to the chair just prior to commencement to clarify any last minute points of concern?
- Has everyone seen and signed the attendance list?
- Do I have a complete and accurate record of all apologies?
- Am I sitting properly with good back support?
- Is my writing arm positioned so as to minimise the stress on my wrist?
- Have I put all distractions out of my mind and am I fully focused on the meeting?
- For each item, am I formulating in my mind an idea as to the main emphasis of the discussion and the possible decisions, from the chair's opening summary?
- Am I working with the chair to ensure that all participants who want to contribute are able to do so?
- Am I getting the sense of the *message* or am I focusing too much on the actual words?
- Am I isolating the key points from each speaker's contribution?
- Am I relating the key points to the central matter under discussion?
- Am I tending to record the arguments verbatim, or am I employing my personalised form of shorthand?
- From the discussion, am I clearly extracting and recording all the decisions and action points?
- For the action points, have I made a note of who is responsible and the deadline date for completion?
- Where points are unclear, am I asking for appropriate clarifications?
- Am I maintaining concentration or is my mind beginning to wander?
- Am I checking periodically that my handwriting is still legible!
- Am I tending to write sentences or am I mastering the use of bullet points and abbreviations?
- Am I setting out my bullet points clearly and legibly in a vertical format with plenty of space in between, or am I tending to bunch them together in clusters?
- If a problem arises regarding understanding and it is inappropriate at that point to seek clarification, have I clearly highlighted this (perhaps with a different colour pen) in my notes?
- Am I moving my writing hand too much (thus contributing to tiredness) or am I moving the *paper* to create the writing space I need?

CHECKLIST continued

- Am I maintaining eye contact with the speaker in order to improve the quality of my listening or do I seldom look up from my notes?
- Am I being influenced or distracted by the voice tone of the speaker, the manner of delivery or the emotional nature of the contributions, or am I still focusing on the key points, actions and decisions?
- Although my notes will be structured to a greater degree during the writing up stage, am I trying to keep the key points to the fore in my note-taking?
- Am I intervening confidently and assertively when required or am I a little 'backward in coming forward'?
- Am I helping the chair to keep the meeting on track and, where necessary, to observe procedural conventions?
- When I am contributing to an item on the agenda, do I ask the chair to summarise the discussion in the interest of an accurate set of minutes?
- Am I *listening* effectively, remembering to employ the different forms of listening in order to create a rounded out understanding?
- Am I allowing anything to influence my listening in a *negative* sense, such as bias, prejudice, cynicism, indignation or vested interests?
- Have I clearly noted the time, date and place of the next meeting?
- Before the participants disperse, am I taking the opportunity to speak to anyone I need to in order to seek necessary clarifications?

CHECKLIST

The minute-taker's reminder checklist: after the meeting

Tick the following as completed:
- Have I taken the trouble to shake hands with and say goodbye to, all the participants or have I remained in my seat with my head in my notes?
- Have I taken the time, after everyone has left, to analyse my notes and check understanding and legibility?
- Have I made sure that all the key points are highlighted while my memory is still fresh?
- Have I thanked the chair?
- Have I discussed any pertinent points with the chair prior to leaving the meeting room?
- Have I asked the chair to sign the minutes of the previous meeting (if necessary) so that they can be filed and archived?
- Have I started writing up the draft minutes as soon as possible after the meeting?
- Am I using the correct format and style having regard to the nature of the meeting and the level of formality or informality required?
- Am I using an appropriate numbering system?
- Am I using the passive voice and correct verbs, particularly where the minutes are of a formal nature?
- Have I checked the level of detail required for this particular meeting? Is the recording of decisions and actions enough or do I need to incorporate the 'flavour' of the discussion?
- When summarising the discussions, am I being crisp and concise, perhaps consolidating certain discussion points into one sentence or is the minute tending to be too drawn out and 'wordy'?
- Have I carefully proof read the minutes before sending them to the chair for approval?
- I am aware that the draft minutes need to be returned on time to adhere to the meeting cycle, but have I given the chair a clear deadline for their approval?
- When sending the minutes have I clearly highlighted the action points for the individual participants?
- Which background papers do I need to file with the minutes?
- From my perspective as minute taker, what went well at the meeting and what areas need to be worked on?
- What exercises can I undertake to practice my listening and note-taking skills?
- At the next meeting, what can I *personally* do to make it even more effective?

Index

Active listening 135–137
    barriers to 136
    four elements 136–137
Agenda 51–61
    any other business 56–59
    circulating 61
    creating 53–54
    creating logical order 54
    deviation from 155
    example 53, 60
    giving notice 52
    good, benefits of 51–52
    good, constructing 52–55
    inclusion of objectives 54–55
    inclusion of timings 55–56
    inviting contributions 52
    main items 112–117
    responsibility for preparation 52–53
    sub-dividing items 54
Annual general meeting 21–22
Any other business 56–59, 117
Apologies for absence 106–108
Argument, minuting 153
Assertiveness 139–141
Away-days 23

Board meetings 22
    who should take minutes 158
Bullet points 157

Chairperson 31–40
    active listener 37
    'after' list 164, 168
    appropriate dress 37
    assertiveness 37
    'before' list 163, 164–165
    capability 34–35
    careful planning 32–34
    conclusion of meeting 38
    conducting brief review with minute-taker 38
    critical evaluation 38–39
    consciousness of body language 37
    dealing with tension and conflict 37–38
    different personality types 35–36
    'during' list 166–167
    effective 32–39
    employ effective questioning techniques 36
    enthusiasm 37
    humour 37
    identifying actions and persons responsible 38
    overview of role 31–32
    patience 37
    provision of frequent summaries 37
    speaking at comfortable volume 37
    summarising decisions reached 38
    taking minutes 160
    understanding role 31–40
Change to minutes 153
Checklists 163–168
Circulating the minutes 119
Committee meetings 22
Communication skills 130
    active listening 135–137
    considering effectiveness of own communication 133–135
    how to be a credible communicator 134–135
    listening skills 137
    understanding and evaluating messages 132–133
    verbal 131, 132
    visual 131, 132
    vocal 131, 132
Completion of actions agreed at meeting 162
Conferences 23
Conflicts of interest 108–109

Declarations of interest 108
Departmental meetings 23
Detailed notes 157

Editing draft minutes 119
Effective note-taking 41–50, 70–84
　abbreviate 76–83
　alternative approach 71–72
　brainstorm additional activities and sub-sets of activities 47
　compile final master list of activities in chronological order 47
　compile list in chronological order 46–47
　create computer-held filing system 43
　create minute-taking strategy map 44–45
　create series of additional reference documents 47–49
　deciding on approach 71
　developing strategy 43–50
　developing strategy for each meeting 42
　establish meeting cycle for each meeting 43–44
　evaluate 73–76
　importance of strategic approach 41–42
　'learn' technique 72
　listen 73
　maintain focus on personal skills development 49–50
　monitor, review and amend 49
　retention of notes 84
　review and note 83–84
　review strategy file for each meeting prior to preparation 49
　spider diagram 82
　step-by-step guide 43–50
　strategy 41–50
　symbols 79
Electronic archiving 128
Emotional intelligence 143–144
Extra detail 160
Extraordinary general meeting 22

Falsification 155
Filing the minutes 120

INFER memory aid 145–147
　execute 146
　finalise 146
　identify 146
　note 146
　reflect 146–147

Job rotation 157–158

Laptop 123–125
　advantages 123–124
　disadvantages 123–124
　writing minutes in meeting 124–125
Layout 101–121
Local authority meetings 22

Management meetings 23
Matters arising 111–112
Meetings 21–30
　agenda items 28
　any other business 28
　apologies for absence 27
　attendance details 65
　attendees 62–63
　basic elements 101
　date of next meeting 28
　effective 24–26
　　factors 25
　equipment 63–64
　final check 65
　formality 28–29
　general administrative arrangements 62–66
　glossary of terms 29–30
　ineffective 24–26
　　factors 25
　information only 28
　introduction 27
　level of detail 116
　matters arising 27
　minutes of previous meeting 27
　necessary paperwork 64
　notice 62–63
　personal preparation 62–69
　rooms checklist 64
　structure 26–28
　types 21–24
　venue 63–64
Minute-taking mix 118
Minutes
　accurate record, as 6–10
　aide-memoire at following meeting 6
　clarity 8
　clutter free 9
　coherence 10
　completeness 8
　compliance 9
　comprehensive historical record 6
　conciseness 7–8
　consistency 8
　correctness 9
　definition 1
　eight Cs 7

INDEX

evidence of decisions taken 2–4
guiding principles 6–10
legal and regulatory framework 4–5
point of reference for those unable to attend 5
prompt to action 6
purpose 2–6
style of writing 10

One-off informal meetings 24
Opinions and emotions 154
Organisational issues 14–16
   asked to perform ancillary activities 15
   decisions and actions unclear 15
   demands from forceful participants 15
   excessive AOB section 15
   excessively long meetings 16
   expectation: every word to be recorded 16
   falsification of minutes by chair 16
   frequent criticism 16
   fussy amendments following draft 16
   ineffective chairperson 15
   lack of appreciation 16
   no provisions of training 15
   perception: anyone can do it 14
   perception: low status function 14
   procrastination by participants 15
   rambling meetings 15
   unclear contributions from participants 15
   unreasonable timescales 16
   unsuitable venue 15
   unsupportive culture 16

Passive voice 154
Personal development plan 147–149
   prompting questions 147–148
Personal issues 16–18
   chairperson difficult to approach 17
   difficulties in completing draft on time 18
   difficulty in composing minutes 18
   difficulty in listening 17
   difficulty in taking notes and contributing 18
   feeling stressed 18
   frequent fatigue 18
   frightened to make mistake 17
   frightened to speak up during meeting 17
   inability to concentrate 17
   lack of knowledge about meeting topics 16
   lack of knowledge about technical terms 16
   lack of minute-taking experience 17
   lacking in confidence 18
   participants difficult to approach 17
   poor summarising skills 18
   tendency to write down everything 17
   too many meetings to minute 17
   unskilled as minute-taker 17
   worried about what other people think 18
Personal preparation 62–69
   arrange writing area 68
   arrive early 69
   assemble all necessary materials 68
   be conversant with meeting rules and procedures 67
   check understanding of technical terms and jargon 66
   create own seating plan 69
   determine layout style for minutes 66
   meet with chairperson prior to meeting 67
   meet with participants prior to meeting 67
   prepare physically and mentally 68
   read all relevant supporting papers 66
   read minutes of last meeting 66
   relationship with chairperson 67
   sit next to chairperson 69
   undertake additional research if required 66
Personal qualities of the proactive minute-taker 139–144
   assertiveness 139–141
   emotional intelligence 143–144
   self-confidence 142
Personal skills development 145–150
Practical exercises for note-taking 149–150
Presentations
   minuting 161
Project team meetings 23
Proofreading 118
Publication of minutes 158–160

Recording devices 125–126
   retention of recordings 126
Retention of board minutes 120
Retention of minutes 155–156, 161–162
Role of minute-taker 11–20
   case analysis 13–14
   challenges 12–18
   dual role 19
   key activities 12
   multi-tasking, advantages and disadvantages 19
   organisational issues 14–16
   organisational problems 12
   personal issues 16–18
   taking notes and contributing in same meeting 19

Safeguards where minutes accessible 158
Self-confidence 142
Skills development 162
Smartpens 126
Status of minute-taker 160–161
Steering group meetings 23
Structure 101–121
  any other business 117
  apologies for absence 106–108
  date of next meeting 117
  declarations of interest 108
  heading 102–104
  listing attendees 104–106
  main agenda items 112–117
  matters arising 111–112
  minutes of previous meeting 109–111
  minuting conflicts of interest 108–109
  naming names 116–117
  numbering of minutes 117–118
  resolution at general meeting 113–115
Style 101–121

Team briefings 24
Technology 122–129
  impact on management of meetings 127–128
  meeting administration, and 128

Transforming notes into minutes 85–100
  avoiding errors 96–97
  checklist of useful phrases 99
  checklist of useful words 98
  choosing appropriate style of minutes 92–94
  developing minute-writing toolkit 97
  list of key points 87
  logical order of content 87
  recording methods 91
  reference material 100
  reported speech 94
  spider diagram 88
  structuring 91
  suggestions for promoting event 87
  summarising 94–96
  summary of streamlining process 92
  techniques for streamlining notes 85–92
  templates 100
  writing style 92
    active 93
    passive 93
Trouble-shooter 152–162

Virtual meetings 127

Word-for-word contribution 152

Lightning Source UK Ltd.
Milton Keynes UK
UKHW051231040719
345496UK00012B/224/P

9 781860 727290